BLACK+DECKE

The Complete Guide to

DECKS

Updated 7th Edition

Featuring the Latest Tools, Skills, Designs, Materials + Codes

COOL
SPRINGS
PRESS

Inspiring | Educating | Creating | Entertaining

Brimming with creative inspiration, how-to projects, and useful information to enrich your everyday life, Quarto Knows is a favorite destination for those pursuing their interests and passions. Visit our site and dig deeper with our books into your area of interest: Quarto Creates, Quarto Cooks, Quarto Homes, Quarto Lives, Quarto Drives, Quarto Explores, Quarto Gifts, or Quarto Kids.

First Published in 2022 by Cool Springs Press, an imprint of The Quarto Group, 100 Cummings Center, Suite 265-D, Beverly, MA 01915, USA. T (978) 282-9590 F (978) 283-2742 QuartoKnows.com

Cool Springs Press titles are also available at discount for retail, wholesale, promotional, and bulk purchase. For details, contact the Special Sales Manager by email at specialsales@quarto.com or by mail at The Quarto Group, Attn: Special Sales Manager, 100 Cummings Center, Suite 265-D, Beverly, MA 01915, USA.

26 25 24 23 22   1 2 3 4 5

ISBN: 978-0-7603-7153-4

Digital edition published in 2022

eISBN: 978-0-7603-7154-1

Library of Congress Cataloging-in-Publication Data available.

Cover Image: Decks by Kiefer, www.decksbykiefer.com, designs@decksbykiefer.com
Page Layout: Megan Jones Design
New Photography: Joseph Truini Photography
Illustration: Christopher Mills, pages 34 and 147

Printed in China

The Complete Guide to Decks, 7th Edition

Created by: The Editors of Cool Springs Press, in cooperation with BLACK+DECKER.

NOTICE TO READERS

For safety, use caution, care, and good judgment when following the procedures described in this book. The publisher and BLACK+DECKER cannot assume responsibility for any damage to property or injury to persons as a result of misuse of the information provided.

The techniques shown in this book are general techniques for various applications. In some instances, additional techniques not shown in this book may be required. Always follow manufacturers' instructions included with products, since deviating from the directions may void warranties. The projects in this book vary widely as to skill levels required: some may not be appropriate for all do-it-yourselfers, and some may require professional help.

Consult your local building department for information on building permits, codes, and other laws as they apply to your project.

Contents

The Complete Guide to
Decks

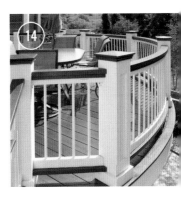

Contents (Cont.)

Introduction

Adding a deck improves the livability of your home because it adds value to a living space. Think of a deck as a room without walls, one that makes the outdoor space more usable and beautiful while providing a transition from the comfort and security of a home's interior to the sunlit natural attraction of the great outdoors. Decks are also wonderful solutions to challenges presented by the terrain, such as thickly shaded, woodsy locations that would not support a vegetable garden or steep slopes that might otherwise be unusable.

Mostly, though, a deck is a stage. It's the platform on which you can engage in your favorite outdoor leisure activities, from barbecuing to dining al fresco, to hot tubbing and stargazing. Simply put, any deck increases the ways in which you enjoy your home and property.

Building a deck that does just what you want it to do begins with a simple assessment of the space where the deck will be placed. That's just where *The Complete Guide to Decks* starts. The next section of this book will help you begin choosing just the right deck for your yard and preferences. You'll first need to determine what restrictions your site imposes and figure out just what size, orientation, and shape best suits your yard, house, and personal relaxation style. Inevitably, this will involve setting a budget. All of that will lead to the most enjoyable part of the project: actually designing the deck. You'll find guidance through each of these steps in the section covering planning and design.

Taking that design from sketch paper to actual structure is where things get more complicated. That's why *The Complete Guide to Decks* leads you through code considerations, material options, and other concerns, such as buying and building green. Even if you're not building the deck yourself, knowing these things will pay off in the long run because you'll be able to confidently communicate with contractors and other deck-building professionals from a vantage point of knowledge.

That's also why, regardless of what role you want to play in the process, you should read through the sections on deck projects and deck plans. You'll learn a lot about the different ways in which decks are equipped with different features such as low-voltage lighting, the right way to build-in seating, and how to prevent deck failures down the line. The book closes with some simple fixes for common deck problems.

All along the way, you'll enjoy detail-oriented photos to show you how things should look when done properly, and many that will simply serve as inspiration for what you want your own deck to look like. Keep *The Complete Guide to Decks* on hand as a reference and you're sure to wind up with a deck that serves as a perfect, custom-made outdoor room for you, your family, and friends.

Gallery of Inspiring Decks

Building a deck is all about choosing the correct options for your situation. And considering the profusion of decking materials, the incredible variety of surface appearances and finishes, the amazing number of features that can be added to modern decks, and the innate flexibility of deck design to conform to even the most unusual yard topography, it should be clear that deck design is limited only by the boundaries of imagination.

However, just starting with a blank piece of paper can be a daunting challenge. A small or large deck? One, two, or three levels? Built-in seating or movable furniture? All of those questions and more need to be answered if you are to create the deck of your dreams, and one that serves all the purposes you hope it will.

Getting started, it always helps to view examples of successful decks. Seeing what others have done to answer their aspirations is a sure way to spur your own creative juices. That's the point of this section. Although these pages may not contain exactly the perfect deck for your yard, home, and family, you will find a range of decks representative of the potential options at your disposal. These should inspire flashes of brilliance in designing your perfect outdoor structure.

Multilevel Decks

Take advantage of a slope with a cascading, multilevel deck design. The redwood used in this deck is a traditional choice because the wood's appearance fits perfectly into the naturalistic surroundings.

NOTE: Many localities require a guard or railing behind built-in benches. Check with your building department.

Make your deck more interesting and more useful by creating activity areas in different parts of the deck. The upper area is used for dining and entertaining, while the lower level extends the living space inside. Placing one area at ground level means the deck does not need a railing, opening up the design.

Planning is crucial to using every part of a multilevel deck to its best advantage. Building a tiered deck involves a lot of expense, so it pays to put careful consideration into the planning phase. Make sure you identify what activity each level of the deck will accommodate. The layout should also be logical. Here, cooking is done nearest the kitchen, with a social area down one platform. A hot tub is positioned at the bottom, level with the pool.

Walkout Decks

Look to an inside corner as the ideal location to nestle a quiet, cozy walkout deck. Landscaping may be used around the deck to help it blend in with the house and yard. Use skirting as the builder did here to hide an unsightly supporting structures and blend it even more into the home itself.

Curve the borders of a walkout deck to make it a much more interesting feature. This deck not only offers eye-catching good looks with the double-curved front edge, but the curving shape is also replicated in darker accent boards run throughout the deck. It's a beautiful way to dress up what could have been a fairly plain outdoor platform.

Jazz up a single-level walkout deck by designing it with an unusual shape. The shape of this outdoor entertaining area adds a little zest to a staid home design, and using white rails and lattice ties the deck in visually with the siding of the house—a technique that can be used with any deck.

Pool Decks

Disconnect the deck from the pool to maintain a platform for keeping watch over watery fun. An elevated deck like this one can be a lovely complement to a pool, especially with the shaded refuge of a pavilion where swimmers can take a break out of the direct sun. As a bonus, parents can keep a watchful eye on children playing in the pool while still relaxing in dry comfort on the deck.

In some cases, it makes sense to combine the pool and the deck into one outdoor living area. Here, the outdoor space is in full view of those in the house thanks to the large sliding glass doors. It's what designers call bringing the outdoors in. The wood decking forms a transition between the indoor rooms and the outdoors.

Spa Tub Decks

Even a relatively small and simply designed deck can be divided into distinct activity areas. The spa forms one area that is separated from the dining and cooking space at the far end of the deck. The built-in benches help tie the two areas together.

The owners of this house wanted a private spa and deck space off a lower-level bedroom, but they also wanted a deck off an upper-level living area. Cedar glulam (glue laminated) beams and joists give the overhead structure the feeling of an arbor rather than the underside of a deck.

Supplement your spa tub. A spa tub can be an amazingly social addition to your deck. Even if visitors don't feel like getting wet, they can interact with bathers in the tub. That means the feature can become the centerpiece of a party—so it's a good idea to design the deck with areas that take advantage of the tub and create interaction across the deck. Note how this spa tub is not actually resting on the deck itself: it is sited on top of a poured concrete pad that is not connected structurally to the deck. Locating a spa tub on a deck requires considerable reenforcement of the undercarriage and is not a recommended DIY project.

Railings and Stairs

Order your curved railings–no fuss, no muss–from composite manufacturers. Composite and other synthetic materials can be formed to many different shapes, opening up the possibility of ordering a rail like this one ready to assemble. The possibilities for including curves along the edge of deck have never been greater.

Opt for metal tube balusters if you want a distinctive look that is relatively easy to assemble. You can choose from the enameled metal shown here, copper, iron, aluminum, or stainless steel. Add white posts and rails to set off the distinctive balusters.

Color your railings and stair treads to go with your deck. The potential inherent in synthetic decking materials includes the possibility of railings colored to meet your specifications. Here, a golden-brown railing perfectly complements the light-colored deck and adds a handsome monochrome element to the entire structure. Although not every color in the rainbow can be crafted in composite or vinyl railing, consider the possibility of unusual hues for a bit of flair.

Most decks have balusters and rails in one form or another, but why not switch it up and try a lattice design for the safety railing? Here, the color complements the darker gray top rail. You can construct your own lattice panels or buy them ready made. They are available in both plastic and natural wood.

A well-designed walkout deck gets a boost from a series of wide, almost platformlike, steps that lead down to a lower level. Built-in low-voltage lighting in the step risers increases safety and adds points of interest at night.

This deck offers amazing views of the surrounding area, and because it is built in California, it has to meet stringent earthquake engineering requirements. Some of the railing uses the same type of siding as the house to tie the deck back to the original structure. The open powder-coated steel grid accentuates the views.

All-metal railings are becoming increasingly popular. Here, the gray and black of the system works well with the color of the decking. And the open design does nothing to obstruct the breathtaking views.

Built-in Features

Plant a design feature on your deck. These composite planters were made to be paired with the cross-brace, legless benches. Built-in deck planters can be simple or ornate, but bringing flora onto the deck is always a great way to integrate the manmade structure into the surrounding landscape.

NOTE: Many localities require a guard or railing behind built-in benches. Check with your building department.

Decorate with an overhang that will draw all eyes up. Pergolas are some of the favorite high-end features to add to a deck. They help define an area of the deck—in this case, a cooking and dining area—and make a huge style statement. They are also adaptable. For instance, you can cover a pergola such as this with fabric "sails" to create a shaded area in an otherwise sunny deck, or even install fiberglass or Plexiglas panels to create an all-weather safety zone.

Add a gazebo for a stunning visual that creates a highly usable outdoor room. These are significant elements to build into a deck, but manufacturers offer complete kits to make the construction somewhat easier and more predictable. Whether you use prefab or custom-build your own gazebo, they are ideal features on medium to large decks.

Built-in Seating

Plan seating into the deck design. Not only do benches serve an incredibly useful and practical purpose, but they can also be stylish focal points. The slotted-seat versions here are popular—in straight runs or the more engaging angled form featured on this deck—because the construction allows for free flow of air and moisture, preventing mold and other detrimental conditions.

Turn to a straightforward, simple bench design for easy-to-add deck seating. The bench can create a visual break at the edge of a low deck as well as introducing a comfortable place to rest. The bench in this case was built from prefab brackets that attach to the deck and make building the benches a quick and easy process. See pages 238 to 243.

A low wall on an upper level serves as the back of built-in seating on a lower level that is three steps down. The end tables provide valuable set-down space, and they echo the planters on the upper level.

BRACING PERPENDICULAR TO B

American Wood Council

(1) 3/8 diameter
thru-bolt with
washers, typical

2x4, typical

beam

2

BRACING PARALLEL TO BEAM

INCHES

1   2

Deck Planning + Design

Building a deck requires many different stages, and none are more important than the planning and designing stages. Get this part right and you are well on your way to building the deck that enhances your outdoor living space, is attractive, and is safe. And a well-designed plan can help you avoid costly, and potentially dangerous, mistakes down the road. To put your best foot forward, plan to spend time at the beginning of the project at a desk developing a thorough plan.

As you begin the planning process, keep in mind that your deck needs to satisfy four goals: it should meet the functional needs of your household, contribute to your home's curb appeal and property value, fit your project budget, and satisfy local building codes for safety. This chapter will help you familiarize yourself with all four goals so you can build confidently and correctly, the first time.

You can design your own custom deck, but there are also many sources for ready-made deck plans, including some in this book, as well as other published deck plans. You may be able to find the perfect deck for your home without designing it from scratch or by making minor modifications to these plans.

In this chapter:
- Evaluating Your Site
- Deck Building Codes
- Determining Lumber Size
- Understanding Loads
- Developing Your Deck Plan
- Working with Building Inspectors

Evaluating Your Site

In many cases, the deck you end up with will depend a great deal on what you start out with. A deck will be affected by sunlight and shade, prevailing winds, and seasonal changes. Those natural factors will influence how and when you use your deck. There are other site-related issues to consider as well. An on-grade deck will reduce the size of your yard–which may or may not be an issue, depending on your desire for a garden, lawn, or play area. A raised deck could be perfect for entertaining friends, but it could also create unwanted shade in a flowerbed or darken a nearby living space.

The size and layout of your property will also impact your choice of a deck site. You may need to build a multilevel deck or a long run of steps to reach the ground of a sloping yard. Will your proposed deck site require you to remove a tree or two to accommodate it, or will you simply build around it? A tall deck could give you new vistas on the neighborhood, but will it encroach on your neighbor's window privacy or put you dangerously close to power lines? These are all factors to keep in mind when settling on the final location of your deck. Make sure the benefits of your deck site outweigh any compromises you may need to make.

The location of your deck is often dictated by the design of your house. In this home, the main living areas are a few feet above the yard level. The short posts raise the level of the deck so that it is easy to reach from the family room inside the house. However, you'll usually have more than one site to choose from, so consider all the options before you commit to a final location for your deck.

Accommodate severe natural yard topography, such as a steep slope, with your deck design. Often, a multilevel deck is the best solution to a sloped yard. You can also use a long staircase with a landing to navigate the vertical rise.

Make room for nature. The more your deck blends with the surrounding landscape, the more natural and beautiful it will appear. Incorporating a tree ring into your deck design is one way to preserve nature, but limit the use of rings to trees that have achieved mature size.

Before you build a second-floor deck, consider whether your site will compromise your or your neighbor's privacy, place you too close to power lines, or shade areas of the yard or windows beneath.

Design a deck to the best advantage of other notable built-in features such as swimming pools. These elements will always influence how you position, site, and construct your deck.

Deck Building Codes

Building codes have evolved and become more stringent in recent years. And deck building codes are no exception. There is good reason for this because an improperly constructed deck can be a safety hazard, eyesore, and can even devalue your home. That's why any deck project should begin with some research into local codes.

Although codes will vary from place to place, most are based on the International Residential Code. Talk to your local building department; most will supply a list of relevant deck-building requirements for your area and will answer questions you might have about compliance on your particular project. If you're using a contractor to build your deck, make sure he or she is up to date on the latest codes. For more information on deck codes and good building practices, go online and download a free PDF copy of "Prescriptive Residential Deck Construction Guide" published by the American Wood Council (See Resources, page 268). It is not the actual building code, but many code requirements are based on this publication.

Post-footing diameter and depth are essential for proper deck support. The requirements differ from locality to locality based on frost level (the footing should be poured below frost level). Be aware that requirements for minimum footing diameter have become more stringent in recent years; footings that support important structural members, such as beams, often need to be 12" or 18" or even wider in diameter. The 8-in.dia. concrete tube forms you see at the building center are best reserved for fence posts.

The following pages show examples of code-compliant building details. This is by no means comprehensive. Always remember that your local building department and its inspectors have the last word on code requirements.

Ledger flashing (usually metal or reinforced plastic) must be positioned according to code—wrapping over the top of the ledger and under the building paper and siding—to prevent water from infiltrating between the ledger and the wall. Many codes require flashing between the ledger and wall as well.

Beam overhangs or "cantilevers" are strictly regulated by code and vary depending on the type of wood and thickness of the beam. Generally, the cantilever should not exceed 1" in length for every 4" of joist span. Your local building inspector will have a table of allowable cantilever amounts based on joist depth, species, and spacing.

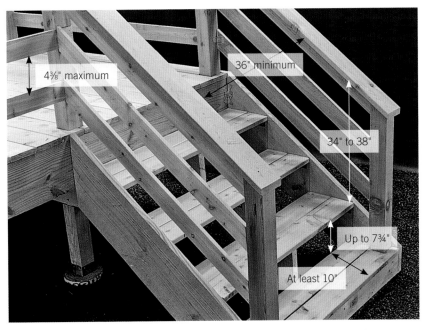

Railings are required by local codes for decks more than 30" above the ground and must usually be at least 36" in height. Bottom rails must be positioned with no more than 4" of open space below them. Balusters, whether vertical or horizontal, can be spaced no more than 4" apart.

Stairs must be at least 36" wide, although 48" is preferable. Vertical step risers should be a maximum of 7¾" high—if left open, the opening must not be greater than 4". (Risers are incomplete in this photo.) Treads should be a minimum of 10" deep. Variation among risers, or among treads, should not exceed ⅜". Railing tops should be 34" to 38" above tread nosings, and a grippable handrail is required for stairs of more than four treads. This staircase, as shown, is incomplete: any staircase with three or more steps must have a graspable handrail (see page 153) and a landing area that is the full width of the stairs and at least 3' from front to back.

Beams must either sit on top of posts in an approved post cap or be notched into a post that is at least 6 × 6. Either 4 × 4 or 4 × 6 lumber can be used for posts 8' high or less (measured to the underside of the beam). Longer posts must be 6 × 6.

Beam assemblies. Built-up deck beams (two or more pieces of dimensional lumber are attached face-to-face) must be fastened together with staggered rows of 10d galvanized nails or 3" deck screws, spaced 16" on center. Beams of three members must be secured from both sides. Exterior construction adhesive is also recommended for the built-up beams.

Deck footing sizes vary and are calculated based on both the load of the deck and the makeup of the soil. Local codes usually specify a formula for calculating post-footing sizes, but bigger is better. Posts can be connected to footings with a post base hardware or sunk into the concrete of the footings. (Generally, a post base is preferred because it eliminates ground contact that can cause the post to rot).

On conventional platform-framed houses, ledgers may be attached directly to the rim joist (also called band joist) with galvanized lag screws or high-strength, self-tapping ledger screws (see page 72) driven in a staggered pattern. On larger decks, additional lateral load connectors often are recommended or required. These connectors secure the outer joists to joists inside the house via a threaded rod. If your home is built with floor trusses or with joists that are parallel to the rim joist, alternate connection methods are likely required—check with your local building department.

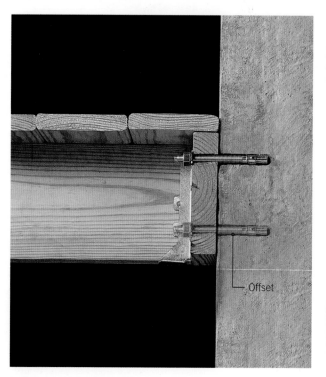

Offset

Ledgers and concrete walls. Ledgers fastened to solid concrete must be attached with bolts and washers driven into approved expansion, epoxy, or adhesive anchors.

Ledgers may not be attached directly to hollow-block foundation walls. This is a new restriction in many areas that previously allowed ledgers to be attached to hollow-block walls with lag screws driven into metal or epoxy anchors.

Notching posts for attachment to a deck joist is no longer allowed. Through-bolts that penetrate the entire post and the joist and are secured with nuts must be used instead. For the most secure attachment, use a metal anchor attached to a perpendicular joist (see page 28, lower left).

Stair lighting. Deck stairs must be illuminated at night from a light located at the top of the landing. The light can be switch-controlled from inside the house, motion-controlled, or used in conjunction with a timer switch.

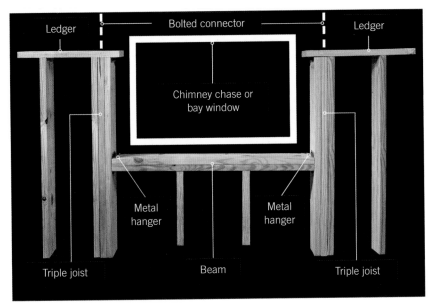

Ledger — Bolted connector — Ledger

Chimney chase or bay window

Metal hanger — Metal hanger

Triple joist — Beam — Triple joist

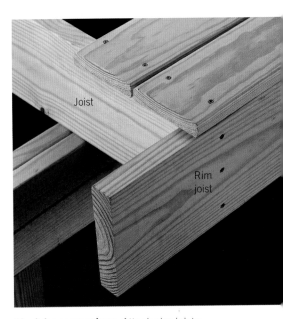

Joist

Rim joist

If your ledger installation area is interrupted by a chimney chase, bay window, or other permanent obstruction, you may frame around that obstruction. The opening generally requires a triple joist on each side. A double or triple beam must be hung between the triple joists (it may not be connected directly to them) at a distance of no more than 3' from the ledger. The ends of the ledger must be secured to the house framing with bolted connectors.

Rim joist connections. Attach rim joists to the end of each joist with a minimum of three #10 × 3" exterior wood screws. Secure the decking to both the rim joist and the perpendicular joist using the same deck screws.

You may toe nail joists to a beam only if the deck is attached to the house. Best practice is to secure joists to the beam using a hurricane clip.

Toenail two 8d nails on one side and one 8d nail on other side

Hurricane clip

Install staggered fasteners on the ledger board using spacing specified in the table below.

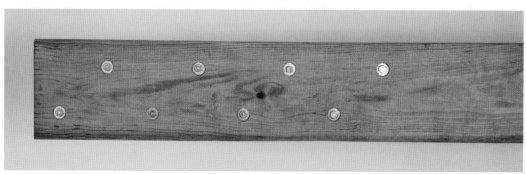

LOCATION OF LAG SCREWS AND BOLTS IN BAND JOISTS AND DECK LEDGER BOARDS

	TOP EDGE	BOTTOM EDGE	ENDS	ROW SPACING
LEDGER	≥ 2"	≥ ¾"	≥ 2" & ≤ 5"	≥ 1⅝" & ≤ 5"
DIMENSION LUMBER BAND JOIST	≥ ¾"	≥ 2"	≥ 2" & ≤ 5"	≥ 1⅝" & ≤ 5"

DECK LEDGER ATTACHMENT USING SCREWS OR BOLTS

JOIST SPAN	≤ 6'	> 6' & ≤ 8'	> 8' & ≤ 10'	> 10' & ≤ 12'	> 12' & ≤ 14'	> 14' & ≤ 16'	> 16' & ≤ 18'
				CONNECTOR SPACING O.C.			
½-inch lag screw with ≤ ½-inch sheathing	30"	23"	18"	15"	13"	11"	10"
½-inch lag bolt with ≤ ½-inch sheathing	36"	36"	34"	29"	24"	21"	19"
½-inch lag bolt with ≤ 1-inch sheathing or ≤ ½" sheathing and ≤ ½ inch stacked washers	36"	36"	29"	24"	21"	18"	16"

The above are requirements specified by the International Residential Code for decks with a live load of 40 pounds per square foot (psf) and a dead load of 10 psf, which is the minimum. Decks engineered for heavier loads, such as those that must hold snow during the winter, will have different requirements. Consult your local building department for specific requirements in your area.

Ledger boards should be pressure-treated lumber that's at least 2 × 8 in size. The ledger board should be the same width as the joists that will be supported by it.

Use the correct-size galvanized steel or stainless steel joist hanger. Attach the joist hanger using the fastener specified by the hanger manufacturer. Install a fastener into every round and oblong hole in the hanger.

One way to attach a beam to a 6 × 6 post is to notch the post and secure the beam using ½" diameter galvanized steel machine bolts and washers. Or, you can mount beams on top of posts with galvanized post cap hardware.

Joists may not be attached to posts with through bolts, even when mortises are cut into the posts to house the joists.

(continued)

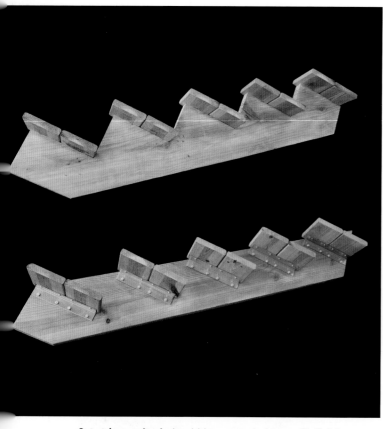

Cut stringers (top) should be supported every 6'. Solid stringers (bottom) should be supported every 13' 3".

Stair stringers require metal hanger hardware, not only nails or screws, when they are attached to a support member.

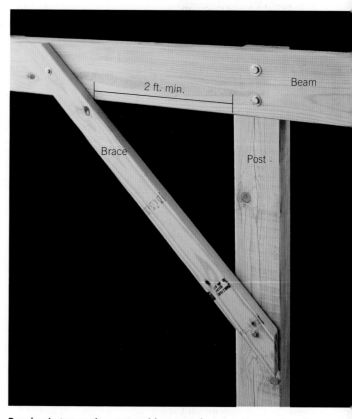

Deck guard support posts should be secured using attachment hardware or wood blocking for long-term strength. See pages 146 to 147 for other attachment options.

Bracing between the post and beam on freestanding decks will reduce movement that can weaken the deck.

Filler strip

Open risers have the potential to trap the head of a small child. Do not allow an open riser to pass a 4" diameter sphere. Install filler strips to reduce riser opening size, beginning with the fourth riser.

DOES SOIL TYPE MATTER?

Some types of soil can withstand more pressure than others. For this reason, tables that list minimum footing sizes are based on different soil types. The photos below show different types of soil. You may need to identify the soil you will be building on when you apply for the building permit. Many deck builders and building officials as-sume soil has a 1,500 psf capacity, but the latest building codes specify different footing sizes for different soils.

Gravel and sandy gravel soils have a presumed 3,000 psf load-bearing capacity.

Sandy soils have a presumed 2,000 psf load-bearing capacity.

Clay and silt soils have a presumed 1,500 psf load-bearing capacity.

Determining Lumber Size

Most decks have several major components, including the ledger, decking, joists, beams, posts, footings, railings, stairway stringers, and stairway treads. To create a working design plan and choose the correct lumber size, you must know the span limits of each part of the deck. The ledger is attached directly to the house and does not have a span limit.

A span limit is the safe distance a board can cross without support from underneath. The maximum safe span depends on the size and wood species of the board. For example, 2 × 6 southern pine joists spaced 16 inches on-center can safely span 9', while 2 × 10 joists can span 14'.

In some designs, deck beams and joists may cantilever past the beam that supports them. To comply with the building code, deck beams can cantilever one-fourth the span of the beam past the end posts. Joists have roughly the same requirement—one-fourth the length of the joist span—but recent changes to the code make some exceptions. Check with your local building department for exact requirements.

Composite, plastic, and aluminum decking all have their own span specifications, which can vary from manufacturer to manufacturer. Always consult the manufacturer's recommendations when using non-wood decking. None of these materials are suitable for use in structural support. In other words, posts, joists, and ledgers will all be wood or, rarely, steel.

Begin planning your deck by first choosing the size and pattern for the decking. Determine the actual layout of joists and beams by using the tables on the opposite page and page 34 as well as span charts from other sources (see page 266) and your local building department. In general, a deck designed with larger lumber, such as 2 × 12 joists and beams, requires fewer pieces because the boards have a longer span limit. Finally, choose the stair and railing lumber that fits your plan, using the same tables.

Use the design plans to make a complete list of the quantities of each lumber size your deck requires. Add 10% to compensate for lumber flaws and construction errors. Both lumberyards and home centers will

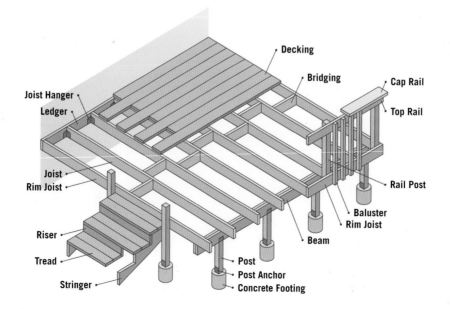

Here are the components most decks contain.

Nominal vs. Actual Lumber Dimensions: When planning a deck, remember that the actual size of lumber is smaller than the nominal size by which lumber is sold. Use the actual dimensions when drawing a deck design plan.

NOMINAL	ACTUAL
1 × 4	¾" × 3½"
5/4 × 6	1" × 5½"
2 × 4	1½" × 3½"
2 × 6	1½" × 5½"
2 × 8	1½" × 7¼"
2 × 10	1½" × 9¼"
2 × 12	1½" × 11¼"
4 × 4	3½" × 3½"
6 × 6	5¼" × 5¼"

WOOD DECKING NOMINAL THICKNESS	INSTALLED PERPENDICULAR TO JOIST		INSTALLED DIAGONAL TO JOIST	
	Single Span *	Multiple Span	Single Span	Multiple Span
5/4 or 1¼"	12"	16"	8"	12"
2"	24"	24"	18"	24"
Non-Wood Decking	Consult Manufacturer's Recommendations		Consult Manufacturer's Recommendations	

*Decking boards supported by two joists are considered single span. Those supported by three or more joists are multiple span.

Recommended Stair Stringer Sizes: Stringers should be spaced no more than 36" apart. Use of a center stringer is recommended for stairways with more than three steps.

SIZE	SOUTHERN PINE			DOUGLAS FIR			REDWOOD/CEDAR		
	12" OC	16" OC	24" OC	12" OC	16" OC	24" OC	12" OC	16" OC	24 OC
2 × 6	9' 11"	9'	7' 7"	9' 6"	8' 4"	6' 10"	8' 10"	8'	6' 10"
2 × 8	13' 1"	11' 10"	9' 8"	12' 6"	11' 1"	9' 1"	11' 8"	10' 7"	8' 8"
2 × 10	16' 2"	14'	11' 5"	15' 8"	13' 7"	11' 1"	14' 11"	13'	10' 7"
2 × 12	18'	16' 6"	13' 6"	18'	15' 9"	12' 10"	17' 5"	15' 1"	12' 4"

The above requirements are for decks designed for a live load of 40 psf. Decks engineered for heavier loads will have different requirements. Consult your local building officials for exact requirements.

Understanding Loads

The supporting structural members of a deck—the posts, beams, joists, and footings—must be sturdy enough to easily support the heaviest anticipated load on the deck. They must carry the substantial weight of the surface decking and railings and also the weight of people, deck furnishings, and, in some climates, snow.

The tables and diagrams shown on the following pages will help you plan a deck so the size and spacing of the structural members are sufficient to support the load, assuming normal use. These recommendations apply to many regions, but you should still check for local regulations that are unique to your area. In cases where the deck will support a hot tub or pool, you should work with a structural engineer to design your deck.

Since different species of wood have different strengths, make sure to use the entries that match the type of lumber sold by your building center. When selecting the size for concrete footings, make sure to consider the composition of your soil.

Joists attached to ledger/bearing on beam (no cantilever): In this simple design, the end of the joist rests on the beam. Table 2 shows how the length of the joist determines the beam span or the spacing of posts that support the beam. So, for a 12' joist, a Southern pine beam made of two 2 × 10s nailed together will have a maximum span of 7' 4" Or will it?

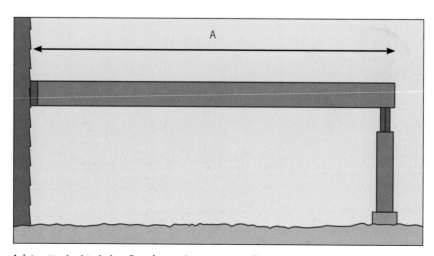

Joists attached to ledger/bearing on beam: no cantilever

TABLE 2: DECK BEAM SPANS OF DOUBLED 2-BY LUMBER

SPECIES	SIZE	JOIST SPANS (FEET)						
		6	8	10	12	14	16	18
		Maximum Deck Beam Spans (feet-inches)						
Southern Pine	2–2 × 6	6' 11"	5' 11"	5' 4"	4' 10"	4' 6"	4' 3"	4'
	2–2 × 8	8' 9"	7' 7"	6' 9"	6' 2"	5' 9"	5' 4"	5'
	2–2 × 10	10' 4"	9'	8'	7' 4"	6' 9"	6'4"	6'
	2–2 × 12	12' 2"	10' 7"	9' 5"	8' 7"	8'	7' 5"	7'
Douglas Fir	2–2 × 8	8' 2"	7' 1"	6' 4"	5' 9"	5' 2"	4' 8"	4' 4"
	2–2 × 10	10'	8' 7"	7' 9"	7'	6' 6"	6'	5' 6"
	2–2 × 12	11' 7"	10'	8' 11"	8' 2"	7' 7"	7' 1"	6' 8"
Redwood/Cedar	2–2 × 6	6' 2"	5" 4"	4' 10"	4' 5"	4'	3' 8"	3' 4"
	2–2 × 8	7' 10"	6' 10"	6' 1"	5' 7"	5' 2"	4' 10"	4' 5"
	2–2 × 10	9' 7"	8' 4"	7' 5"	6' 9"	6' 3"	5' 10"	5' 6"
	2–2 × 12	11' 1"	9' 8"	8' 7"	7' 10"	7' 3"	6' 10"	6' 5"

Live load: 40 psf; dead load 10 psf. Attaching two lengths of 2-by lumber is a common way to construct deck beams, but there are others, such as using three boards nailed together. The beam span requirements change with different configurations. Check with the building department to get the exact requirements for your area. The requirements will also be different if your deck must support heavier loads, such as those produced by snow.

This table and those found in the IRC model code assume that all joists cantilever the maximum one-fourth the length of the joist. The table's calculations reflect a 3' cantilever for our 12' joist. That affects the load and the beam span. To correct the problem, the industry came up with a set of modifiers. For joists with no cantilever, multiply the length of the joist by 0.66. So, 12 multiplied by 0.66 equals 7.92. Now, look at the 8'-joist span column. The double 2 × 10 beam now has a maximum span of 9'.

Joists attached to ledger/bearing on beam (with cantilever): As mentioned above, Table 2 assumes that the joists cantilever the full one-fourth their length. If that is your design, the table is a good resource. If the cantilever is shorter, use these values to adjust the joist length for this table: for a cantilever of $\frac{1}{12}$ the joist length multiply by 0.72, $\frac{1}{10}$ by 0.80, $\frac{1}{8}$ by 0.84, $\frac{1}{6}$ by 0.90.

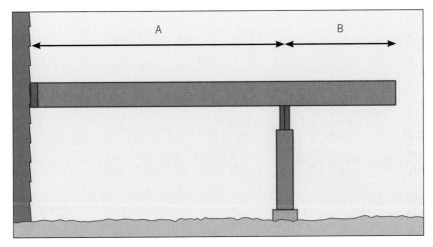

Joists attached to ledger/bearing on beam: with cantilever. (Not drawn to scale.)

Choosing footing sizes: A deck's footings are concrete pads that are buried beneath the surface of the deck. A pier, also made of concrete, connects the footing to the posts that support the deck's beam. Together, they provide a firm foundation for the deck.

The size of the footing is determined by the tributary area it supports. Think of it this way: Each deck support, which are the footings and the ledger, is responsible for a specific area of the deck, which is the load imposed by the deck that is half the distance to the next support. Refer to the Tributary Zones illustration. You will need to find the area of each zone. So, if the beam is 8 feet from the house, the ledger attached to the house will cover the first 4'. The area for Zone A is 4 × 10 (the width of the deck), or 40 square feet.

Do the same for the other Zones. First, divide the distance between posts in half, so half of 3' 6" (or 3½') is 1¾'. You must include the cantilevers. Add 1.75 to the cantilever of 1' 6" (1½') to get 3.25 for the width of Zone B. Determine the length by adding 4 and 2 for a length of 6'. (The dimensions for Zone D are the same in this illustration.) The area for Zones B and D is 6 times 3.25, or 19½ square feet each.

Find the area of Zone C by multiplying 3.5 times 6, or 21 square feet. The end tributary areas tend to require smaller footings than those in the middle of the deck. Then compare your findings to Table 3 to determine the size footing that is necessary. In this simple example, the footing sizes will be about the same, but often end tributary areas can require smaller footings than those located in the middle. Most builders use the largest footings for the entire deck.

All footings must be buried at least 12" below the surface. But in areas where frost heave—the freezing and thawing of the soil—occurs footings must be buried below the frost line, sometimes as deep as 36" or more.

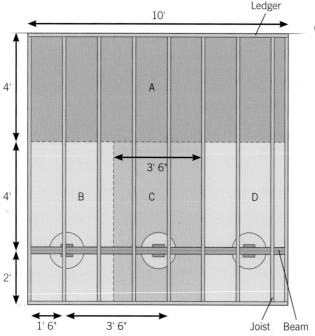

Tributary zones to determine footing size.

TABLE 3: MINIMUM FOOTING SIZES— 40 PSF LIVE LOAD DECKS

TRIBUTARY AREA IN SQUARE FEET	SIDES OF SQUARE FOOTINGS	DIAMETER OF ROUND FOOTINGS	THICKNESS OF FOOTINGS
5	7"	8"	6"
20	10"	12"	6"
40	14"	16"	6"
60	17"	19"	6"
80	20"	22"	7"
100	22"	25"	8"
120	24"	27"	9"
140	26"	29"	10"
160	28"	31"	11"

The above requirements are for decks built on soil that has a 1,500 psf, the lowest bearing capacity. Other types of soil will have different requirements, as will decks built to withstand heavy snow loads.

Developing Your Deck Plan

Begin the design process by making a list of the things you want to do on the deck. Will there be a cooking and dining area? Space to entertain friends? Will it be a private sanctuary where you can decompress? These answers will help determine the size, shape, and location of your deck. Consider how the features of the house and yard influence the deck design. Weather, time of day, and seasonal changes affect deck usage. For example, if your deck will be used mainly for summertime evening meals, look at the sun, shade, and wind patterns on the planned site during this time of day.

Of course, building plans also help you estimate lumber and hardware needs, and provide the measurements needed to lay out the deck and cut the lumber. Keep in mind that lumber comes in even 2-foot intervals. Order the right lengths to keep cutting and waste to a minimum.

You will need two types of drawings for your deck plans and to obtain a building permit. A plan view shows the parts of the deck as they are viewed from directly overhead. An elevation shows the deck parts as viewed from the side or front.

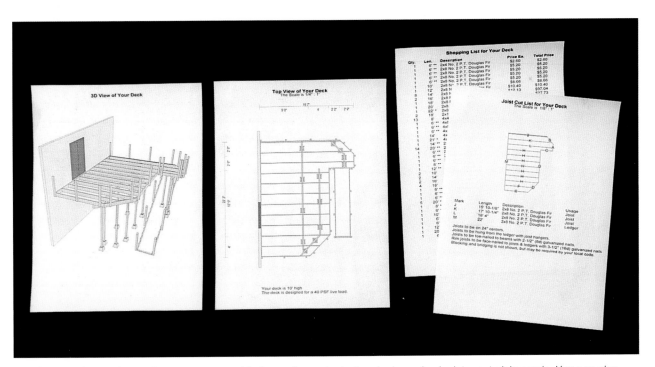

Decking suppliers and some home centers provide free software to design decks and calculate materials needs. You can also purchase software created specifically for deck design to get a 3D perspective on what your new deck will look like.

HOW BIG SHOULD MY DECK BE?

One of the first questions homeowners have to grapple with is the size of the new deck. It helps to think about how the deck relates to the house and how you plan on using the space.

The deck should be in proportion to the house it is attached to. The deck's size should not overwhelm the house nor should it be so small that it gets lost, or worse, it does not give you the outdoor space you wanted. Some professional designers believe that the deck should not be larger than about 20 percent of the square footage of the house. If you are planning a deck made up of different sections, no one section should be larger than the largest room in the house.

The way you plan on using the deck will influence its overall size. Here are some starting points to consider: A seating area will require about 150 to 250 square feet, an outdoor kitchen with a dining table will need about 300-plus square feet; and walkways that connect one section with another should be at least 6 feet wide.

Many decks are broken up into sections. One way to create a new area is to add another level, say one that is three steps up from another section. When changing levels, use multiple steps. One lone step can become a tripping hazard.

 ## How to Create Design Drawings

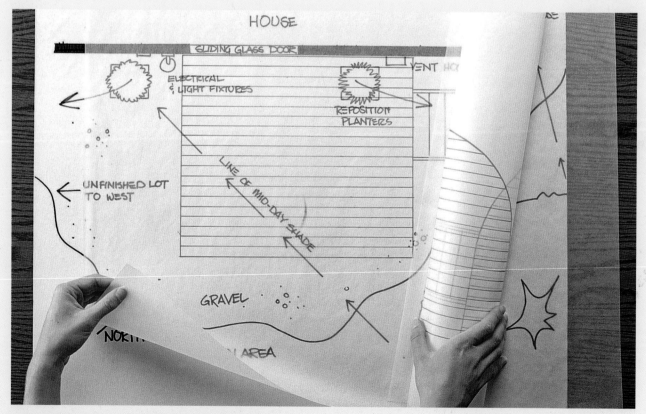

Use tracing paper to sketch different deck layouts. Then, test your ideas by overlaying the deck sketches onto a drawing of your building site. Make sure to consider sun patterns and the locations of existing landscape features when developing a deck plan.

Adapt an existing deck plan, either borrowed from a book or magazine, or purchased in blueprint form. Tracing paper, pens, and measuring tools are all you need to revise an existing deck plan.

Use drafting tools and graph paper if you are creating a deck plan from scratch. Use a generous scale, such as 1" equals 1', that allows you to illustrate the deck in fine detail. Remember to create both overhead plan drawings and side elevation drawings of your project.

If you prefer working on computer to drafting by hand, you can choose from a number of different computer-aided design (CAD) programs specifically developed to help the homeowner design his or her own deck and landscaping. Although most of these programs are sophisticated and powerful, they are generally easy to learn and use. Most include tutorials, and it generally takes only a few hours to become proficient with the software. These programs are loaded with features to help you envision and create a deck customized for your house. They include the ability to accurately re-create the exterior structure of your home and rough elements in the landscape. You can create and view both plan-view and elevation perspectives, and materials lists. The majority of these type of programs include the possibility of outputting drawings suitable for submission to building departments. But beyond the pragmatic uses, the best of these allow you to develop amazingly realistic renderings of material color and texturing, and give you the option of trying out different features such as cable railings or skirting. Some even offer 3-D perspectives that can be rotated on screen. Prices range from free to more than $200—buy the software that matches your needs and will work on your current computer.

The plan drawings produced by some CAD programs are acceptable to many local building departments.

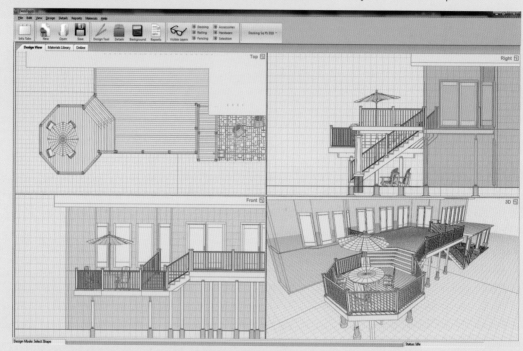

CAD programs have come a long way, and many can now show rotatable 3D versions of your deck design.

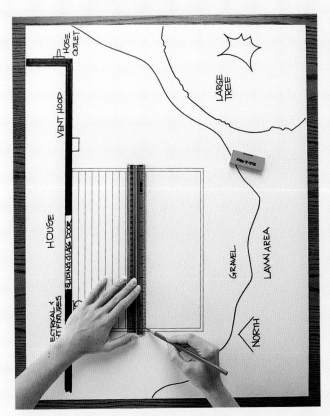

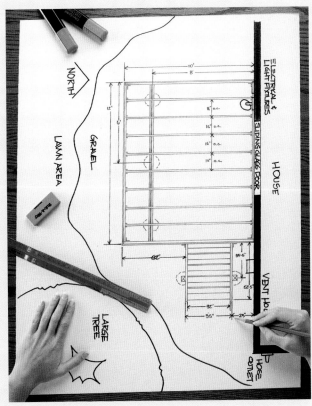

To avoid confusion, do not try to show all parts of the deck in a single plan view, especially for a complicated or multilevel deck. First, draw one plan view that shows the deck outline and the pattern of the decking boards. Then make another plan view (or more) that shows the underlying ledger, joists, beams, and posts.

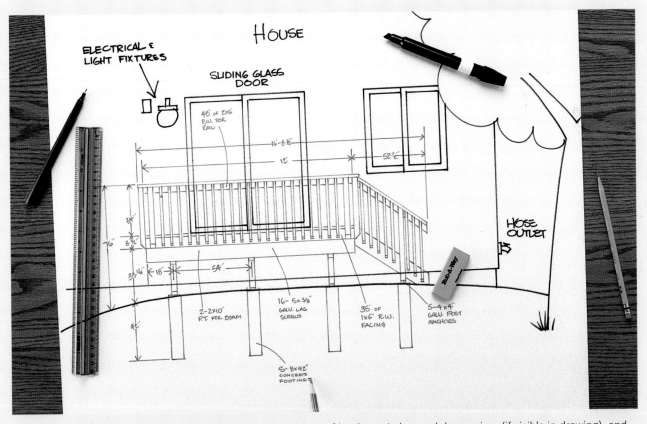

Elevation drawings must include deck dimensions, size and type of hardware to be used, beam sizes (if visible in drawing), and footing locations and their dimensions. Also indicate the grade of the ground in the deck area. Make multiple elevation drawings if necessary for complicated or multilevel decks.

Working with Building Inspectors

Most parts of the country will require you to obtain a building permit for your deck, especially if it is more than 30 inches off the ground. The permitting process starts with you contacting the building department to find out what is required of you. In most cases, you will need to submit multiple copies of your building plan. Be sure to find out how many copies you will need.

These pages show some of the most common code requirements for decks. But before you design your project, check with the building inspection division of your city office, since code regulations vary from area to area and are updated frequently. Local officials will supply updated code requirements for your municipality.

Once you have completed your deck plans, return to the building inspections office and have the official review them. If your plans meet code, you will be issued a building permit, usually for a small fee. This process often takes a few days to a few weeks, depending on the locale. Regulations may require that a field inspector review the deck at specified stages in the building process. If so, make sure to allow for the review schedule in your project schedule.

While it might be tempting to forge ahead with your deck design and bypass the building inspector entirely, it's a big mistake. Building a deck without the proper permits can lead to fines, and you may even be required to tear the deck down or significantly rebuild it to satisfy local codes. Do the right thing: consider permits and inspections to be a necessary part of the construction process.

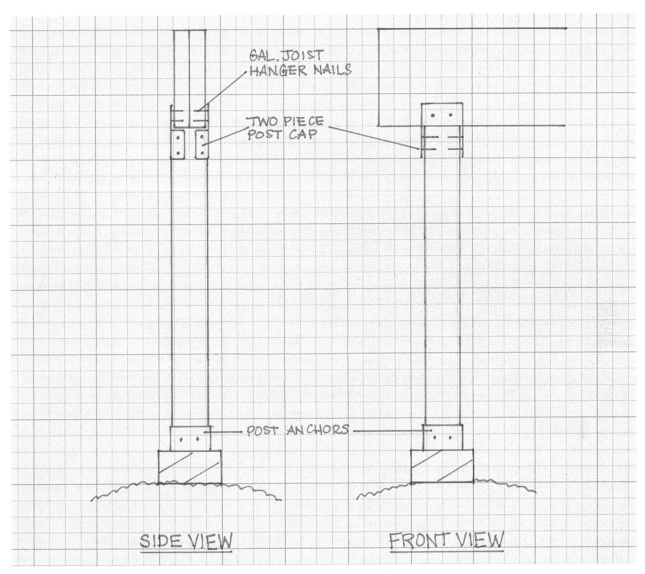

GAL. JOIST
HANGER NAILS

TWO PIECE
POST CAP

POST ANCHORS

SIDE VIEW

FRONT VIEW

Draw detailed illustrations of the joinery methods you plan to use for all structural members of your deck. Your building official will want to see details on post-footing connections, post-beam joints, beam-joist joints, and ledger connections. Be prepared to make adjustments.

PLAN-APPROVAL CHECKLIST

When the building official reviews your deck plans, he or she will look for the following details. Make sure your plan drawings include all this information.

- Overall size and shape of the deck.

- Position of the deck relative to buildings, property lines, and setbacks. Generally, a deck must be at least 5 ft. from the property line, although this varies locality to locality.

- Location of all beams and posts.

- Detailed drawings of joinery methods for all structural members of the deck.

- Size and on-center (OC) spacing of joists.

- Height of deck above grade.

- Thickness of deck boards—or profile of composite decking.

- Type of soil that will support the concrete post footings: sand, loam, or clay.

- Species of wood to be used, and/or type of composite material.

- Types of metal connectors and other hardware you plan to use in constructing the deck.

- Lighting and other electrical outlets or fixtures that will be wired into the deck.

Deck Materials + Tools

This chapter will help you become familiar with the variety of materials and tools you will need to build your deck. You'll need forms, concrete and gravel for making footings, treated posts and framing lumber for the deck's undercarriage, an assortment of connective hardware and fasteners, flashing supplies, decking, and materials for building railings and stairs. Get ready to make some long shopping lists! You may also want to acquaint yourself with the deck-building section of your local home center and the supplies and services your local lumberyard can offer before you start your deck project. That way, you'll be able to find what you need quickly and easily when you really need it.

If you're a seasoned do-it-yourselfer or woodworker, you may already own most of the hand and power tools you'll need for building a deck. You'll also need a few masonry tools. Be sure to review the specialty tools (pages 60 and 61) that you may want to rent for your deck project. They can help you work smarter, not harder.

In this chapter:
- Structural Lumber
- Wood Decking
- Nonwood Decking
- Fasteners + Hardware
- Metal Connecting Hardware
- Screws + Nails
- Flashing
- Footings
- Specialty Tools

Structural Lumber

Even if you plan on using redwood, cedar, or an imported hardwood for the decking surface, pressure-treated lumber is the preferred choice for deck posts, beams, and joist framing. It offers good resistance to decay and insect infestation, it's widely available in most parts of the country and it's a cheaper alternative to other rot-resistant wood species such as cedar or redwood. Treated lumber is milled in 4 × 4, 4 × 6, and 6 × 6 sizes for posts. Larger dimensions are available by special order. You'll need 2× treated lumber for beams and joists. Joists are usually 2 × 8 or larger. If your deck is particularly large or designed with oversized spans, you may need to use engineered beams instead of building beams from treated lumber. Consult with a structural engineer.

Select the flattest structural lumber you can find, free of splits, checks, and large loose knots. To prevent warping, stack and store it in a dry place or cover it with a tarp until you need it. Check the grade stamps or the stapled tags on your pressure-treated posts; they will indicate suitable applications: either above ground or ground contact.

CHEMICAL FORMULATIONS OF PRESSURE-TREATED LUMBER

There was a time when treated lumber was treated with chromated copper arsenate (CCA). But because the formulation contained arsenic, the process was discontinued. Two alternative chemical treatments are now used instead: alkaline copper quaternary (ACQ) and copper boron azole (CBA). Both ACQ and CBA provide wood with the same protection from decay and insect attack as CCA; however, the treatments are more corrosive to metals. Make sure to choose fasteners and connective hardware that are approved for use with ACQ- and CBA-treated lumber.

Treated lumber is available in common nominal sizes for use as deck beams and joists. Choose the clearest, flattest boards you can find, free of checks and splits. Use the correct post size for the deck you are building. Take care not to confuse treated landscape timbers with structurally rated posts. An 8 × 8 landscape timber may look plenty beefy, but it is not rated for structural use unless it has a structural grade stamp.

Lumber for Building Decks

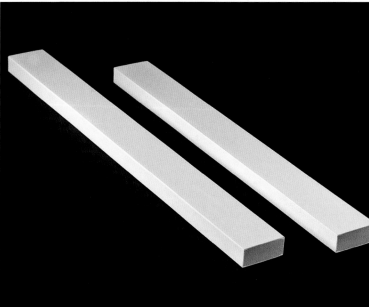

Engineered beams that are rated for exterior use are a sturdy alternative to beams made from 2× lumber. They may be required if you are building a large deck with expansive or unusual spans. Consult with an engineer when using engineered beams.

Composite and PVC lumber is widely used for nonstructural purposes such as decking, skirting, and railing. Made from sawdust, recycled plastic or other synthetic materials, and binders, composite and PVC lumber is available in solid, hollow, and other profiles.

 SEALING END GRAIN

Seal cut edges of all lumber, including pressure-treated wood, by brushing on clear liquid sealer-preservative. Chemicals used in pressure treatment do not always penetrate completely. Sealer-preservative protects all types of wood from rot.

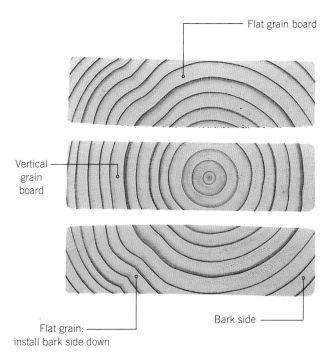

Flat grain board

Vertical grain board

Flat grain: install bark side down

Bark side

Check end grain of decking boards. Boards with flat grain tend to "cup," and can trap standing water if not installed properly. Research studies indicate that flat grain boards cup toward the bark side (not away from it, as was previously thought in the industry), and they should be installed so the bark side faces down.

Wood Decking

While prices can fluctuate wildly from time to time, wood continues to be the most popular choice among decking materials. Pressure-treated decking remains the least expensive deck option, but other types of hardwoods and softwoods feature unique grain pattern and coloring that makes them consistently desirable. Wood of all types is easy to work with, and most softwoods take stain or paint well, allowing you to alter the appearance almost at will.

The two most popular choices for wood decking are pressure-treated and cedar. Depending on where you live, you may have other options as well. Redwood may still be available if you live on the West Coast, and cypress is common in the South. Redwood, cypress, and cedar are naturally resistant to decay and insects, which makes them excellent choices for decking. You can apply finish if you like, or leave them unfinished and they'll weather to a silvery gray color in a few years. If cost is less important than quality, you might consider covering your deck with mahogany, ipê (pronounced "ee-pay") or any of several other exotic hardwoods. These woods are so dense that it is necessary to predrill fasteners during installation.

For pressure-treated or cedar decking, you'll have to select a thickness that works for your budget and design. One option is to use 2× lumber. It will span wider joist spacing without flexing, but generally 2× lumber is made from lower-grade material that may contain more natural defects. Another choice is to use 5/4 decking, pronounced "five quarter." Its actual dry thickness is 1 inch and the edges are radiused to help minimize splinters. Often, 5/4 lumber is clearer than 2× lumber, but it's not as stiff. You may need to space your joists more closely with 5/4 decking. Either way, you can commonly find 2× or 5/4 decking in lengths up to 16 or even 20 feet at most home centers.

Ipê

Cedar

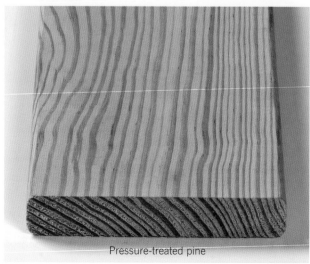

Pressure-treated pine

Wood Decking

Both 2× and 5/4 lumber are suitable for use as decking. However, 5/4 will generally be of higher quality and the radiused edges prevent splintering—an important consideration for bare feet or if you have young children.

If you hand-select each of your deck boards, look for pieces with vertical grain pattern (left in photo). They'll be less inclined to cup and warp than flat-grain lumber (right), but the wood tends to be significantly heavier.

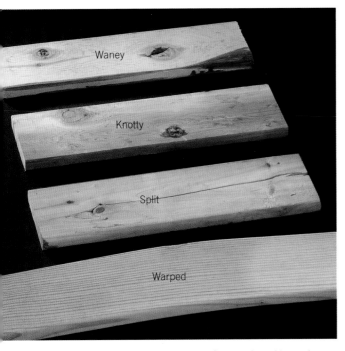

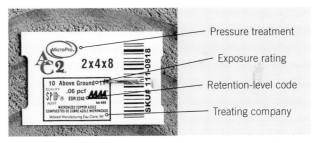

Pressure-treated lumber stamps list the type of preservative and the chemical retention level, as well as the exposure rating and the name and location of the treating company.

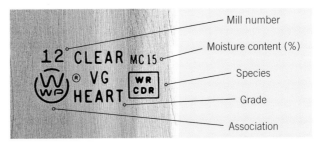

Be picky about the quality of the decking you buy. Natural defects in the wood could make the piece harder to install or deteriorate prematurely. Watch for soft pockets of sap in the wood. Sap will get sticky in warm weather, and the resin can bleed through wood finishes, leaving brown stains.

Cedar grade stamps list the mill number, moisture content, species, lumber grade, and membership association. Western red cedar (WRC) or incense cedar (INC) for decks should be heartwood (HEART) with a maximum moisture content of 15% (MC15).

Nonwood Decking

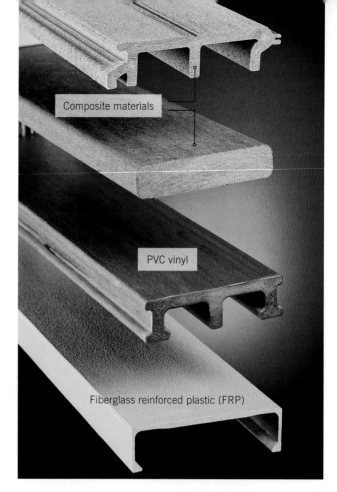

Composite materials

PVC vinyl

Fiberglass reinforced plastic (FRP)

Synthetic alternatives to wood decking continue to grow in popularity thanks to ever-increasing stain- and scratch-resistance, durability, ease of installation, and realistic representations of the look and feel of both softwood and hardwood surfaces.

Most composite decking is a proprietary combination of post-consumer plastic, wood waste, and binders. The plastic makes composite decking impervious to rotting, and insects don't like it. PVC decking is made from polyvinyl chloride and is even more durable than composite products, although slightly more expensive and available in fewer surface appearances. Some decking, known as "capped composites," provide the best of both worlds—a composite core wrapped in PVC.

Decking made from marine grade aluminum is also available. This is easy to maintain, and because it dissipates heat quickly, it remains cool to the touch.

These products are increasingly fade resistant, although almost all of them will fade to one degree or another over time and with direct sun exposure. They are also water-resistant, and some formulations of synthetic decking are even designed for use in sustained direct contact with water. Synthetic decking includes warranties ranging from 10 years on the low end to limited lifetime on the high side. A 15-year warranty is common, and many warranties are transferrable from one homeowner to the next.

Although they are more durable than ever, the biggest new developments in synthetic decking have been in appearance. Both composites and PVC decking are produced in looks and textures that quite convincingly mimic specific softwoods and even hardwoods. Synthetic decking can also be manufactured in colors to match a homeowner's specific needs or design goals. Most synthetic decking is easy to cut, drill, or modify, and can be used most anywhere wood decking might be installed. (Composite and PVC decking is more flexible than wood and may require closer joist spacing; check with the manufacturer.) Maintenance is limited to periodic cleaning.

 SYNTHETICS

Composite materials blend together wood fibers and recycled plastics to create a rigid product that, unlike wood, will not rot, splinter, warp, or crack. Painting or staining is unnecessary. Like wood, these deck boards can be cut to size, using a circular saw with a large-tooth blade.

PVC vinyl and plastic decking materials are shipped in kits that contain everything necessary to install the decking other than the deck screws. The kits are preordered to size, usually in multiples of the combined width of a deck board and the fasteners.

Fiberglass reinforced plastic (FRP) decking will last a lifetime. Manufacturers claim that the material is stronger than wood and not affected by heat, sunlight, or severe weather. The decking is preordered to size, but if necessary, it can be cut using a circular saw with a diamond-tip or masonry blade. FRP decking, however, is considered unattractive and unpleasant underfoot, and is consequently rarely used for residential decking.

Surface patterns and textures of composite or PVC decking range from virtually smooth to intricate wood grain styles. Patterns and textures vary by manufacturer, but many offer varieties that convincingly mimic species of wood, including hardwood.

Synthetic decking colors cover the spectrum of wood tones, plus grays and white. The color is continuous throughout the material, but exposure to strong, direct sunlight may cause the surface color to fade.

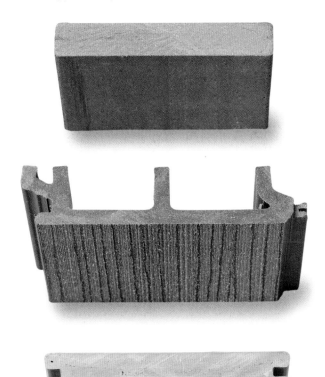

While composite decking can be fastened down conventionally with screws, you may be able to use various edge-fastening systems instead, to avoid driving screws through the board faces. For more on these options, see pages 118 to 123.

Composite and other nonwood decking often requires special fasteners that are designed to reduce "mushrooming" that occurs when the decking material bulges up around the screwhead. Pilot holes are recommended for some types as well.

Fasteners + Hardware

Galvanized or stainless steel lag bolts and washers are the correct fasteners for installing ledgers to the band joist of a house. You can also use them for making other wood-to-wood connections.

Certain structural connections of your deck will require the use of lag screws, through bolts, and concrete anchors to withstand the heavy loads and sheer forces applied to a deck. Attaching ledger boards to your home's band joist, fastening beams to posts, or anchoring posts to concrete footings are all areas where you'll need to step up to larger fasteners and anchors. Be sure to use hot-dipped galvanized or stainless steel hardware to prevent rusting or corrosion from pressure-treating chemicals. Building codes require that you install a washer beneath the heads of lag screws or bolts and another washer before attaching nuts. Washers prevent fasteners from tearing through wood and secure hardware under stress.

Another fastening option to consider is high-strength epoxy, applied from a syringe. If you are fastening deck posts or ledger boards to cured concrete, the epoxy will bond a threaded rod permanently in place without needing an additional metal anchor.

Here is an overview of the anchoring fasteners you may need for your project.

Anchoring Fasteners

Use through bolts (usually lag bolts) to fasten horizontal members to posts. If nuts and washers will be exposed and visible, drill counterbores for them. Otherwise, do not counterbore: the more wood you leave intact the stronger the connection will be.

J-bolts, embedded in the wet concrete of deck footings, provide a secure connection for attaching concrete footings to metal connecting hardware.

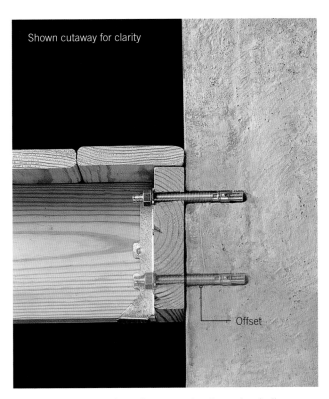

Shown cutaway for clarity

Offset

Wedge or sleeve anchors draw a wedge through a hollow sleeve, expanding it to form a tight fit in solid concrete. A nut on the threaded end holds the ledger boards in place. Do not install fasteners directly above or below one another.

Ledger screws, also called structural screws or construction screws, are a relatively new fastener option. Most local codes now allow them. They are made of high-strength steel and, even though they are smaller in diameter than a typical lag screw, they have greater tensile strength and excellent holding power. Plus, they are self-tapping and have a small head that is easy to work around when locating joist hangers. Many pros now use them, though they are relatively expensive.

Recent code requirements call for changes in how guard rail posts are connected to the deck. Simply bolting the post to the rim joist is no longer acceptable. Now, the force normally exerted on the guard rail post must be transferred to the deck's joist, as shown here. Note the use of a metal tension tie and extra blocking to support the inside post.

High-strength epoxy and threaded rod are good options for attaching metal connecting hardware to concrete footings.

Metal Connecting Hardware

Sheet-metal connecting hardware comes in assorted shapes and styles. It is used to create strong wood-to-wood or wood-to-concrete joints quickly and easily. For instance, metal post anchors not only provide a simple way to attach posts and footings, they also create space between the two surfaces so post ends stay dry. Joist hangers are a fast way to hang long, heavy joists accurately. Post beam caps, T-straps, and angled joist hangers are ideal solutions for building stacked joints or when space doesn't allow you access to drive screws or nails from behind the joint.

Make sure to buy hot-dipped galvanized or stainless steel connecting hardware. Some styles are designed for interior use only and do not have adequate corrosion protection. The product label should identify whether or not the hardware is suitable for pressure-treated wood and outdoor use. Use joist hanger nails made from the same material as the hardware.

Deck post ties fasten stair or railing posts to stringers or joists without through bolts. Hardware is manufactured in 2 × 4, and 4 × 4, 4 × 6, and 6 × 6 sizes.

Framing anchors can be used to fasten rim joists together at corners or make other right-angle attachments, such as stair stringers to rim joists.

NOTE: If you plan to use angle brackets for any connections in your deck, choose your brackets very carefully according to the manufacturer's specifications. It is very easy to select an unendorsed bracket that looks similar, which could cause your deck project to fail an inspection.

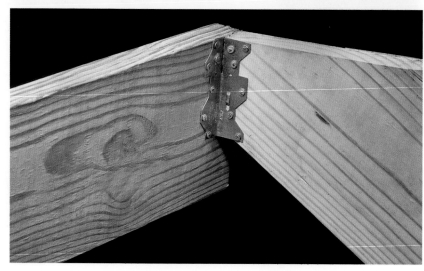

Hanger Hardware for Decks

Post anchors hold deck posts in place and raise the base of the posts to help prevent water from entering the end grain of the post.

Joist hangers are used to attach joists to the ledger and header joist. Double hangers are used when decking patterns require a double-width joist.

Angled joist hangers are used to frame decks that have unusual angles or decking patterns.

Stair cleats support the treads of deck steps. Cleats are attached to stair stringers with ¼ × 1¼" galvanized lag screws.

(continued)

Post-beam caps secure beams on top of posts and are available in one-piece or adjustable styles.

H-fit rafter ties attach 2× joists or rafters to the top of a beam between beam ends.

Hurricane ties are not technically designed for use on decks (they are typically used to help secure rafters), but they may be used to reinforce joist/beam connections if you are concerned about uplift. The connection should still be toe-nailed according to the normal nailing schedule.

Skewable joist hangers attach 2× lumber, such as stair stringers, to the face of framing at an adjustable angle.

Skewable angle brackets reinforce framing connections at angles other than 90° or at beam ends where 45° joist hangers won't fit. Skewable joist hangers that adjust in angle are made for this purpose too, and many pros prefer them.

Direct-bearing footing connectors attach beams directly to footings on low profile decks.

T-straps reinforce the connection between beam and post, particularly on long beams requiring spliced construction. Local building codes may also allow their use in place of post caps.

Strapping plates, also known as nailing plates or mending plates, are useful for a variety of reinforcement applications. They are meant for supplementary use, not to be the only connector.

Screws + Nails

When you attach the beams and joists of your deck, and probably the decking as well, you'll need a collection of screws and/or nails to get these jobs done. It may not seem like screw and nail technology would ever change all that much, but in fact there are many new products available for making these essential connections. If you build your deck from pressure-treated lumber, be sure to use stainless, hot-dipped galvanized steel, or specially coated fasteners that are approved for use with the more corrosive ACQ and CBA wood preservatives. Spiral or ring-shank nails will offer better holding power than smooth nails. Use screws with auger tips and self-drilling heads to avoid drilling pilot holes. Some screws are specially designed for installing composite decking. They have a variable thread pattern that keeps the heads from mushrooming the surrounding material when driven flush.

Whether you are fastening framing together or installing deck boards, your screw options include stainless steel or galvanized. You can also buy screws with colored coatings formulated to resist corrosion from pressure-treated wood. Stainless or coated screws will prevent black staining that can occur on cedar.

If you are building a large deck, consider using a pneumatic nailer with collated nails instead of hand nailing. Collated screws are a faster way to lay deck boards than driving each screw individually. Here's an overview of your fastener options.

Screws + Nails for Decks

Use stainless steel or hot-dipped galvanized framing nails to assemble beams and joists. Install metal connector hardware with 8d or 10d hot-dipped galvanized metal connector nails.

For large deck projects, galvanized pneumatic nails or coated, collated screws are a faster way to fasten framing and decking than driving each nail or screw by hand.

2½" LIGHT REDWOOD

FREE Square Driver Bit!

350 SCREWS FOR 100 SQ. FT. OF DECKING

COMPOSITE DECK SCREW
TrapEase®

No Rusting or Streaking

ACQ Approved

Faster. Easier. Stronger.
FasTen MasTer

NO MORE MUSHROOMS

Many composite decking manufacturers supply special screw types that hold the material in place better than ordinary screws would, and that are colored to match the decking boards.

Make sure your fasteners will resist the corrosive effects of today's pressure-treating chemicals. Fastener manufacturers will usually provide this information on the product label.

If you'd prefer not to see screwheads in your decking but still want to drive them from the surface, you can buy screws with snap-off heads. A special tool breaks the head off after the screw is driven. The resulting hole is much smaller than a screwhead.

Choose your nails and screws carefully. Screws with "bright" or black-oxide coatings and uncoated nails will not stand up to exterior use or pressure-treating chemicals. Fasteners are as crucial to your deck's long-term durability as the quality of the framing lumber or decking.

Flashing

Building codes require that a deck's ledger board be attached directly to wall sheathing and house framing, and that a corrosion-resistant flashing material be used at any junction between a deck ledger and a house. If your home is sided, you'll need to remove the siding in the ledger board area before attaching the ledger to the house. Be sure to install 15# or 30# building paper or self-sealing and adhesive-backed membrane behind the ledger to prevent moisture damage. Rotting in the area behind the ledger is one of the leading causes of premature deck deterioration. Flashing is particularly important if there's no housewrap behind the siding. Once the ledger is in place, cap it with a piece of galvanized Z-flashing, tucked behind the siding, for added protection.

Although building codes don't require it, you may also want to wrap the tops of beams, joists, and posts with self-sealing membrane to keep these areas dry and rot-free. Ledger flashing, self-sealing membrane, and building paper are available at most home centers and lumberyards. They're little details that can make a big difference to the longevity of your deck.

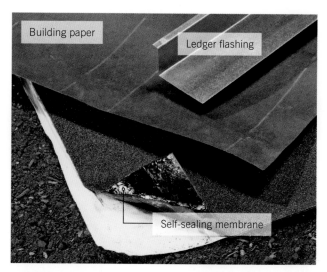

Building felt, also called building paper, is used behind house siding materials. Use it to replace felt damaged during a ledger installation. Ledger flashing, or Z-flashing, prevents moisture damage behind the deck ledger. Self-sealing membrane provides extra protection from moisture in damp climates or in areas where there is snow accumulation. It can be used over flashing or on top of beams, joists, and posts (see below left), and it self-seals around nails or screws that pierce it.

To apply self-sealing membrane, cut a piece to size and position it over the application area. Starting at one end, begin removing the thin plastic backing that protects the adhesive. Firmly press the membrane in place as you remove the backing, working along the installation area. To install long pieces of membrane, enlist the aid of a helper.

Install self-sealing membrane behind the ledger as protection from moisture. You can apply the membrane over the house wrap or building felt or directly to the wall sheathing using the same method shown at left.

Footings

Footings anchor a deck to the ground and create a stable foundation for the posts. They transfer the weight of the deck into the soil and prevent it from heaving upward in climates where the ground freezes. (See page 34 to determine footing sizes.) Generally, footing forms are made from long, hollow tubes of fiber-reinforced paper in several diameters. Once a tube footing is set into the ground below the frostline, you backfill around the outside with soil, tamp it down firmly, and fill with concrete. Metal connective hardware embedded in the concrete will attach the footings permanently to the deck posts.

For soils that have a poor bearing capacity, or if you are building a particularly large deck, you can also

Lumberyards and building centers will stock hollow footing forms in various diameters. The diameter you need will depend on the size and weight of your deck. Your building official will help you determine the correct size when you apply for a building permit.

buy plastic footing tubes with flared bases that bear heavier loads. Or, you can attach a flared footing to the bottom of a conventional tube. For low-profile decks that aren't attached to a house, you may be able to use precast concrete footings instead of buried piers. These footings simply rest on the surface of the soil.

Precast concrete footings are usually acceptable for building low-profile, freestanding decks. Notches on top of the pier are designed to hold joists without fasteners or other hardware.

Cut away for clarity

When building heavy decks or placing footings in unstable, loose soil, you may need to use piers with flared footings. Some styles are molded in one piece, or you can attach a flared footing to a conventional footing form with screws.

Specialty Tools

A big deck project can be labor-intensive and time consuming. Certain specialized tools, such as a power auger, hammer drill, or collated screw gun, can speed tasks along and save you some of the sweat equity involved. But these tools can be expensive, and they're hard to justify buying unless you plan to use them often. Renting them may be a better option. A wide assortment of tools, including the ones on these pages, are available at rental centers at a reasonable cost. Renting gives you an opportunity to try a tool that you're considering buying or use and return a tool you would never consider buying.

A post level (top) is a quick and simple way to check plumb and mark a level cut line on an individual post. A tripod-mounted laser level such as the one shown here (bottom) can help you determine post and footing positions and mark multiple posts at once. The difficulty with using a laser level outside is that the laser is sometimes hard to see. That's why professionals often use detectors that use audible tones to help you align the laser on multiple posts. Tripod laser levels are expensive but handy—if you're building a small deck, it may make sense to rent rather than buy.

A collated screwgun speeds up the process of fastening decking to joists, and it can save wear and tear on your knees. These tools accept strips of exterior screws, and an advancing mechanism allows you to drive them one after the next without stopping. An adjustable clutch prevents the screws from being overdriven.

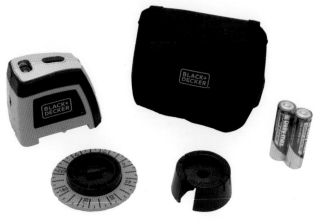

Hammer drills combine the usual rotary action with forward motion, similar to a tiny jackhammer. They make it much easier to drill large pilot holes in concrete or block walls for installing ledger board anchors.

If you have more than a few holes to dig for your deck footings, especially when they're deep, rent a power auger. Both one-person and two-person models are available. A gas-powered engine drives the auger to excavate these holes quickly.

Cordless impact drivers can make quick work of laborious tasks like driving lag screws. Because they have a percussive motion as well as high-torque spinning motion, they leverage two forces at once. They are excellent for driving lag screws as well as deck screws.

Tools for straightening deck boards are relatively inexpensive and allow you to work with bowed boards. The better solution is to return bowed deck boards and install straight ones.

HOW TO BUILD A DECK

Building a Deck: A Step-by-Step Overview

Deck-building is a project you'll tackle in stages, no matter what deck design you choose. The photos on these next four pages provide an overview of the primary stages involved in a typical deck project. The chapters that follow will explore each of these stages in depth.

In this overview, an old, worn deck is replaced with a slightly larger new deck with approximately 180 square foot of outdoor living space (not including the steps). As decks go, it's average in size and the structural techniques are standard. The deck is supported by a ledger board attached to the rim joist of the home, and three main posts set atop large concrete footings. A second set of smaller posts supports the stairs. The 2 × 2 railing balusters are custom-cut on site and topped with a 2 × 6 cap. The structural elements are all made with pressure-treated pine; the decking and the more visible lumber is also pressure-treated pine, but it is precolored to a cedar tone so it does not require a finish coating.

An average-size deck built with standard construction practices is still a major undertaking. Be sure to plan well and arrange for plenty of help at key points, such as when digging and pouring the footings and installing the central beam. In most areas any deck attached to the home requires a building permit issued by your municipality, and there likely will be several on-site inspections required. For this deck, inspection of the footing holes was needed to confirm that they are sufficiently wide and that they extended past the frostline (here, a minimum of 42 inches deep). An additional inspection was done once the undercarriage was completed (before the decking was installed), and a final inspection also was required.

Before

Install a ledger to anchor the deck to the house and to serve as reference for laying out footings (pages 70 to 77), (pages 78 to 83). Use batterboards and mason's strings to pinpoint the right locations for the footings, and check to make sure the layout is square by measuring the diagonals (page 83).

Pour concrete post footings (pages 84 to 88), and install metal post anchors (pages 90 to 95). Set and brace the posts, attach them to the post anchors, and mark the posts for cutting at the point where the beam will be attached. *(continued)*

Fasten the beam to the main posts with post caps (pages 98 to 100). Install the outside joists and the header joist, using galvanized nails. Measure between the outer rim joists and then cut and install a front rim joist parallel to the ledger.

Install the internal joists using metal joist hangers at the ledger (pages 102 to 107). Attach the other ends using hangers or nails according to your approved plan.

Lay decking boards, and trim them to length after installation (pages 109 to 117). If desired for appearance, clad the structural members with fascia boards (page 114).

Build the deck stairs (pages 125 to 133). If three or more stairs are built, a grippable handrail is required.

Install a railing around the deck and stairway (pages 135 to 165). A railing adds a decorative touch and is required on any deck that is more than 30" above the ground.

Structural Support

Regardless of the deck design you choose, every permanent deck has a fundamentally similar structure. Posts and footings anchored in the ground, working in tandem with a ledger board fastened to the house, support a framework of beams and joists that form a deck's undercarriage. Decking, railings, and steps are added to this platform to make it accessible and safe. There are proven techniques for installing each of these structural elements, and that's what you'll learn in this chapter. Once you get comfortable with these skills, you'll be able to apply them to any of the deck projects featured in this book—or create your own unique deck plans.

Following this chapter, we'll also show you important variations to basic techniques you may need to apply to your project, depending on the size, height, or location of your new deck or the topography of your yard.

In this chapter:
- Installing a Ledger
- Locating Post Footings
- Digging + Pouring Footings
- Installing Posts
- Installing Beams
- Hanging Joists

Installing a Ledger

The first step in building an attached deck is to fasten the ledger to the house. The ledger anchors the deck and establishes a reference point for building the deck square and level. The ledger also supports one end of all the deck joists, so it must be attached securely to the framing members of the house.

For all deck ledgers, make sure to use hot-dipped, galvanized lag screws and washers to attach the ledger to the house. Ordinary zinc-coated hardware will corrode and eventually fail if placed in contact with ACQ pressure-treating chemicals. For additional strength on large decks—and where the framing structure will permit it—use through bolts instead of lag screws, tightening down with a washer and nut on the opposite side. Install the ledger so that the surface of the decking boards will be at least 1 inch below the indoor floor level. This height difference prevents rainwater or melted snow from seeping into the house. Deck fasteners and flashing must be installed precisely according to code. Make sure you know what local codes require and follow them to the letter when installing the ledger.

A deck ledger (shown in cross section) is usually made of pressure-treated lumber. Lap siding is cut away to expose sheathing and to provide a flat surface for attaching the ledger. Galvanized flashing tucked under siding prevents moisture damage to wood. Countersunk ½ × 4" lag screws hold the ledger to the header joist inside house. If there is access to the space behind the header joist, such as in an unfinished basement, attach the ledger with carriage bolts, washers, and nuts.

TOOLS + MATERIALS

For all surfaces:		Optional:
Pressure-treated lumber	Z-flashing (galvanized steel or plastic)	Wood chisel
2 × 4s for braces	Level	Metal snips
Drill and bits	Circular saw	Awl
Galvanized (triple zinc plated) lag screws and 1⅜" washers	Caulk gun	Rubber mallet
Silicone caulk	8d galvanized common nails	Masonry anchors for ½" lag screws (for masonry walls)
Pencil	Hammer	Ear and eye protection
	Ratchet wrench or impact driver	Work gloves

How to Cut Out Siding for a Ledger Board

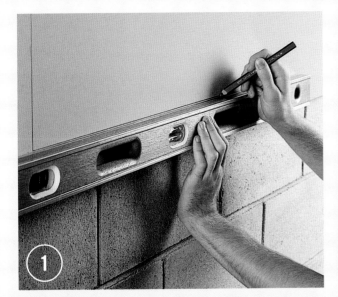

Draw an outline showing where the deck will fit against the house, using a level as a guide. Include the thickness of the outside joists and any decorative facing boards that will be installed.

Cut out the siding along the outline, using a circular saw. Set the blade depth to the same thickness as the siding, so that the blade does not cut into the sheathing.

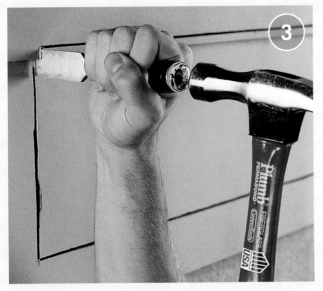

Use a chisel to cut the siding at the ends of the cutout or anywhere the circular saw cannot reach. Hold the chisel with the bevel side facing into the cutout area. Use a claw hammer to pry off the siding and a pry bar as necessary to pop stubborn nails holding siding over the cutout area.

Measure and cut the ledger from pressure-treated lumber. Remember that the ledger will be shorter than the overall length of the cutout.

SIZING YOUR LEDGER OPENING

A wood ledger board should be made from 2× stock that is pressure treated or naturally rot resistant. Pressure-treated pine is by far the most common material. The ledger should be at least a 2" × 8" width, but it cannot be narrower than the joists that hang from it. Best practice is to use lumber of the same dimension as the joists. When sizing the ledger length, be sure to allow for the metal joist hanger flanges at the end—add at least an inch or two per end for nailing the hangers.

TO COUNTERBORE OR NOT TO COUNTERBORE?

Should you counterbore the guide holes for lag screws when attaching a ledger? Good question. Traditionally, many deck builders and DIYers have employed counterbores so the lag screw head is recessed and out of the way of any joist hangers. Some think the appearance is neater too. But today, just about any inspector will tell you not to use counterbores. They base this on the fact that when structural members are tested to determine attachment protocols, they test the full thickness of the lumber. If counterbores are used, the thickness of the board at the point of attachment is reduced and you are actually weakening the holding power. A 2 × 8 with a ½" deep counterbore, for example, will have only 1" of wood at the point of attachment. The counterbore also provides unnecessary exposure and creates a spot for moisture to pool.

Self-tapping ledger screws do not require pilot holes or washers and have low-profile heads so they do not interfere with joist hanger installation.

If you are concerned about having exposed lag screw heads, you may counterbore the lags screws as in the project seen on these pages. But it's a good idea to decrease the spacing between fasteners to compensate. And be sure to fill the counterbores with silicone caulk after the lags are driven.

A third option for attaching ledgers is to use self-tapping ledger screws, which are now allowed by most codes. Typically smaller in diameter and featuring star-drive screw heads, these fasteners can be driven directly into the ledger and rim joist with no pilot holes. They are made from high-strength metal that outperforms the steel used in inexpensive forged lag screws. The low-profile screw heads do not interfere significantly with hanger installation. If you wish to use these screws, check with your building inspector first and confirm which size screw they recommend.

How to Attach a Ledger to a Rim Joist

Remove the old ledger board if you are replacing a deck. Also inspect and remove any deteriorated wood in and around the ledge installation area. If you are installing a deck where none was previously, create a cutout in the siding (see previous page).

Install a backing of building paper and a moisture barrier in the ledger opening, making sure the material is securely tucked behind the siding and it extends past the gap where the rim joist meets the foundation wall. Tuck Z-flashing (galvanized steel or plastic) behind the siding to create coverage for the top of the ledger. Overlap vertical joints in the flashing by at least 4". Friction-fit the flashing only—do not penetrate it with fasteners.

Position the ledger board in the opening, propping it from below with 2 × 4 braces to hold it in place. Tack the ledger in place with 8d galvanized nails.

Attach the ledger board with lag bolts or screws. National building codes require ½" dia. fasteners. The lags should be installed in pairs with the fasteners offset so they are not aligned. Spacing should be according to the approved 16" schedule for your deck. If you are counterboring for the lags (See Sidebar, previous page) drill the counterbore first (top photo) and then the guide hole (bottom).

Attach the ledger to the wall with lag screws or bolts and washers, using a ratchet wrench and socket or an impact driver, following the schedule for your deck.

Seal around the lag screw heads with silicone caulk. Also seal the crack between the wall and the sides and bottom of the ledger. Apply a full bead of the silicone caulk between the top of the Z-flashing and the top of the cutout in the siding.

How to Attach a Ledger to a Masonry Foundation Wall

Measure and cut the ledger. The ledger should be slightly shorter than the overall length of the outline. Mark and drill ½"-deep counterbores (1⅜" dia.) for the lag screws you'll use to attach the ledger, according to your plan. Drill the counterbore first and then drill the smaller guide holes for the lag screw shanks.

Draw an outline of the deck on the wall, using a level as a guide. Center the ledger in the outline, and brace in position. Mark the pilot-hole locations on the wall using an awl or nail. Remove the ledger.

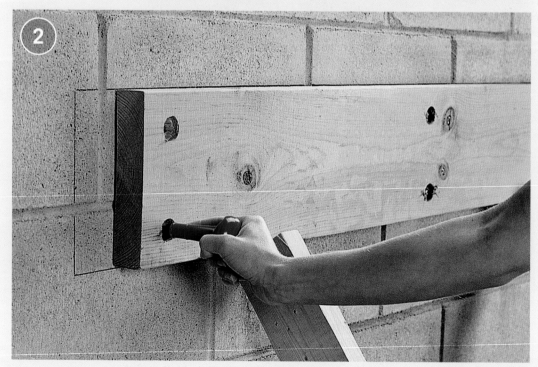

Drill anchor holes 3" deep into the wall using a masonry bit large enough for the anchors.

Drive lead masonry anchors for ½" lag screws into the holes using a rubber mallet.

Attach the ledger to the wall with ½ × 4" lag screws and washers, using a ratchet wrench or impact driver. Tighten screws firmly, but do not overtighten.

Seal the cracks between the wall and ledger with silicone caulk. Also seal the lag screw heads.

How to Attach a Ledger to Metal or Vinyl Siding

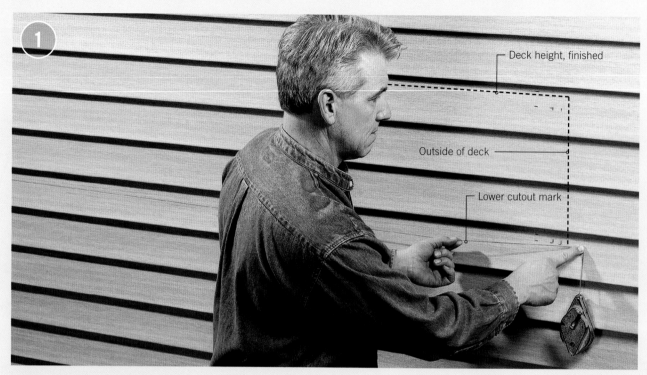

Deck height, finished

Outside of deck

Lower cutout mark

Mark the length of the ledger location so the ledger is aligned with the rim joist of the house behind the siding. Allow for fascia board thickness if it will be added, and create space for metal rim-joist hangers. Then mark the top and bottom edges of the ledger at both ends of its location. Snap lines for the ledger position between the marks. Check the lines for level and adjust as necessary. You may be able to use the siding edges to help determine the ledger location, but only after checking to see if the edges are level. Don't assume siding is installed level.

Set the circular saw blade depth to cut through the siding. Use a metal cutting blade for metal siding; a 40-tooth carbide blade works well on vinyl siding. Cut on the outside of the lines along the top and sides of the ledger location, stopping the blade when it reaches a corner.

Snap a new level line ½" above the bottom line and make your final cut along this line. This leaves a small lip of siding that will fit under the ledger.

Complete the cuts in the corners using tin snips on metal siding or a utility knife on vinyl siding. An oscillating saw also may be used.

Insert building felt underneath the siding and over the existing felt that has been damaged by the cuts. It is easiest to cut and install two long strips. Cut and insert the first strip so it is underneath the siding at the ends and bottom edge of the cutout and attach it with staples. Cut and insert the second strip so it is underneath the siding at the ends and top edge of the cutout, so that it overlaps the first strip by at least 3". Add moisture-barrier flashing.

Cut and insert galvanized flashing (also called Z-flashing) underneath the full length of the top edge of the cutout. Do not use fasteners; pressure will hold the flashing in place until the ledger is installed.

Cut and install the ledger board (see pages 70 to 71).

Locating Post Footings

Establish the exact locations of all concrete footings by stretching mason's strings across the site. Use the ledger board as a starting point. These perpendicular layout strings will be used to locate holes for concrete footings and to position metal post anchors on the finished footings. Anchor the layout strings with temporary 2 × 4 supports, called "batterboards." You may want to leave the batterboards in place until after the footings are dug. That way, you can use the strings to accurately locate the J-bolts in the concrete.

Mason's strings stretched between the ledger and the batterboards are used to position footings for deck posts. Use a plumb bob and wire flags or stakes to mark the ground at the exact centerpoints of footings. Always double check your measurements at this point because any variations can have critical consequences for the rest of the construction.

How to Locate Post Footings

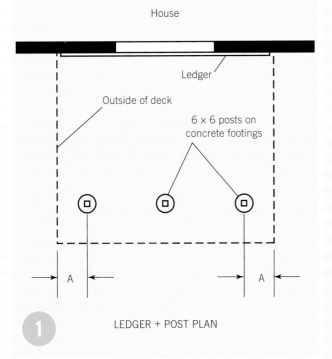

1

LEDGER + POST PLAN

(diagram labels: House, Ledger, Outside of deck, 6 × 6 posts on concrete footings, A, A)

Use your design plan to find distance (A). Measure from the side of the deck to the center of each outside post. Use your elevation drawings to find the height of each deck post.

2

Cut 2 × 4 stakes for batterboards, each about 8" to 12" longer than post height. Trim one end of each stake to a point using a circular saw. Cut 2 × 4 crosspieces, each about 2' long.

3

Assemble the batterboards by attaching crosspieces to the stakes with 2½" drywall screws. Crosspieces should be about 2" below the tops of the stakes.

4

Transfer measurement A (step 1) to the ledger, and mark reference points at each end of the ledger. String lines will be stretched from these points on the ledger. *(continued)*

Drive a batterboard 6" into the ground, about 2' past the post location. The crosspiece of the batterboard should be parallel to the ledger.

Drive a 10d nail into the bottom of the ledger at the reference point (step 4). Tie a mason's string to the nail.

Extend the mason's string so that it is taut and perpendicular to the ledger. Use a framing square as a guide. Secure the string temporarily by wrapping it several times around the batterboard.

Check the mason's string for square using the "3-4-5 method." First, measure along the ledger 3' from the mason's string and mark a point, using a felt-tipped pen.

Measure the mason's string 4' from the edge of the ledger, and mark with masking tape.

Measure the distance between the marks. If the string is perpendicular to the ledger, the distance will be exactly 5'. If necessary, move the string left or right on the batterboard until the distance between the marks is 5'.

Drive a 10d nail into the top of the batterboard at the string location. Leave about 2" of nail exposed. Tie the string to the nail.

(continued)

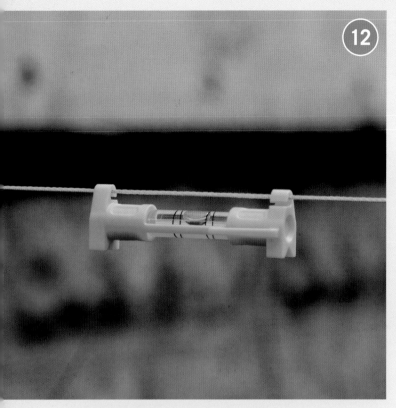

Hang a line level on the mason's string. Raise or lower the string until it is level. Locate the other outside post footing, repeating steps 5 to 12.

Measure along the mason's strings from the ledger to find the centerpoint of the posts. Mark the centerpoints on the strings, using masking tape.

Drive additional batterboards into the ground, about 2' outside of the mason's strings and lined up with the post centerpoint marks (step 13).

Align a third cross string with the centerpoint marks on the first strings. Drive 10d nails in the new batterboards, and tie off the cross strings on the nails. The cross string should be close to, but not touching, the first strings.

16

Check the strings for square by measuring distances A-B and C-D. Measure the diagonals A-D and B-C from the edge of the ledger to the opposite corners. If the strings are square, measurement A-B will be the same as C-D, and diagonal A-D will be the same as B-C. If necessary, adjust the strings on the batterboards until they are square.

17

Measure along the cross string and mark the centerpoints of any posts that will be installed between the outside posts.

18

Use a plumb bob to mark the post centerpoints on the ground, directly under the marks on the mason's strings. Drive a stake into the ground at each point. Remove the mason's strings before digging the footings.

Digging + Pouring Footings

Concrete footings provide solid support for deck posts. Check your local codes to determine the size and depth of footings required for your area. For all but the smallest decks and some stairways, today's codes usually specify that post footings be at least 16 inches in diameter. In cold climates, footings must be deeper than the soil frost line, which can be as deep as 48 inches in some parts of the continental U.S. To help protect posts from water damage, footings are generally poured so that they are at least 2 inches above ground level. You can create footings by pouring concrete directly into a hole with a form on top to create the aboveground portion, or turn to the more common solution of a tube-shaped form that allows you to pour the post you need quickly and easily.

Before digging, consult local utilities for the locations of any underground electrical, telephone, or water lines that might interfere with footings. You can call 811, a national clearinghouse number, which will route you to your local utilities.

TOOLS + MATERIALS

Power auger and/or posthole digger	Utility knife
	Concrete tube forms
Tape measure	Concrete (dry bagged
Shovel	mix or readymix)
Reciprocating saw or handsaw	J-bolts
	Wheelbarrow
Torpedo level	Scrap 2 × 4s
Masonry hoe	Ear and eye protection
Trowel	Work gloves
Plumb bob	

Post-hole diggers are relatively inexpensive and extremely useful. Digging a large deck footing hole will take a long time, but you can work at your own pace. You can also make the hole any size you wish (power augers are limited to three or four standard bit sizes).

A power auger can be a terrific timesaver, but using one is still a very labor-intensive job—especially if the soil in your project site is full of rocks or roots. With the exception of very loose soil, using a two-person auger generally requires that you raise the tool up and down in the hole as you dig, which takes a good deal or teamwork and some brute strength. Even lifting the auger out of a 4'-deep hole is strenuous enough that good back support is highly recommended, as is hearing protection.

One-person power augers are available for rent, but if your hole is 12" or wider in diameter you'll need a two-person tool because you generally can't get bits bigger than 8" for one-person augers.

How to Dig + Prepare Holes for Footings

Dig holes for post footings with a clamshell digger or power auger, centering the holes on the layout stakes. For holes deeper than 35", use a power auger.

Measure hole depth. Local building codes specify depth of footings. Cut away tree roots, if necessary, using a pruning saw.

Pour 2" to 3" of loose gravel in the bottom of each footing hole. Gravel will provide drainage under concrete footings.

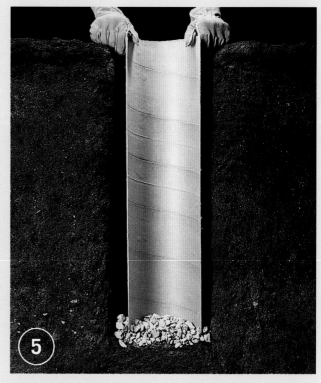

Add 2" to hole depth so that footings will be above ground level. Cut concrete tube forms to length, using a reciprocating saw or handsaw. Make sure the cuts are straight.

Insert the tubes into footing holes, leaving 2" of the tube above ground level. Check the tops of the tubes for level and adjust as necessary. Pack soil around the tubes to hold them in place.

How to Mix Concrete by Hand

Empty one or two bags of dry concrete mix into a wheelbarrow or a mortar box.

NOTE: Concrete is sold in both 60- and 80-pound bags so be sure to use the correct bag size when calculating how much you'll need. Blend the dry mix with a masonry hoe to break up any hard clumps.

Form a hollow in the center of the dry mix, and slowly pour a small amount of water into the hollow. Blend it in using the masonry hoe. Be sure to wear protective gloves and a dust mask.

Add more water gradually, mixing thoroughly until the concrete is firm enough to hold its shape when sliced with a trowel.

How to Mix Concrete with a Concrete Mixer

Fill a bucket with ¾ gal. of water for each 80-lb. bag of concrete you will use in the batch for most power mixers, three bags is a workable amount. Pour in half the water. Before you start power mixing, carefully review the operating instructions for the mixer.

Eye protection

Particle mask or half-mask respirator

Add all of the dry ingredients, and then mix for 1 minute. Pour in water as needed until the proper consistency is achieved and mix for 3 to 5 minutes. Pivot the mixing drum to empty the concrete into a wheelbarrow. Rinse out the drum immediately.

How to Pour Concrete Footings in a Tube Form

Dig postholes and insert a concrete tube form of the correct size (page 86). Some building inspectors want to measure the depth of at least one unfilled footing hole. Check with your building department for requirements. The tube form should be stabilized and level, with the top at least 2" above grade. An easy way to stabilize it is simply to drive a single drywall screw through the inside surface of the form and into scrap 2 × 4 braces. You can also backfill around the form with dirt, but it's better to do this after the concrete footing is dry so you can properly tamp the backfill dirt without worrying about damaging the tube form or knocking it out of level. Use a shovel to slowly guide the concrete into the tube form. Fill about half of the form, using a long rod to tamp the concrete, filling any air gaps in the footing. Then fill the form to the top, crowing it slightly.

Use a 2 × 4 scrap as a screed to strike off excess concrete and create a relatively smooth surface. The concrete still should crown slightly in the form—this allows it to shed water once it is cured.

Insert a J-bolt at an angle into the wet concrete at the center of the footing.

NOTE: If you are pouring multiple footings (normally the case) double-check the location and alignment of the J-bolts compared to your layout lines. Adjust the J-bolts if necessary by resetting them.

(4)

Lower the J-bolt slowly into the concrete, wiggling it slightly to eliminate any air gaps and let the concrete fill back in around the bolt shank.

TIP: Wrap a little duct tape around the threaded end of the bolt to protect the part that will be exposed from the wet concrete.

Set the J-bolt so ¾" to 1" is exposed above the concrete.

(5)

Suspend a plumb bob from your layout lines (re-tie them if you had to remove them to excavate the holes) and confirm that the J-bolts are still in proper location and alignment.

(6)

(7)

Use a torpedo level to make sure the J-bolt is plumb. If necessary, adjust the bolt and repack the concrete. Let the concrete cure, then cut away the exposed portion of tube with a utility knife if its appearance bothers you. Backfill around the footing with dirt, tamping it into the hole with the end of a 2 × 4 as you fill.

Installing Posts

Posts support the deck beams and transfer the weight of the deck, as well as everything on it, to the concrete footings. They create the above-ground foundation of your deck. Your building inspector will verify that the posts you plan to use are sized correctly to suit your deck design.

Choose post lumber carefully so the posts will be able to carry these substantial loads for the life of your deck. Pressure-treated lumber is your best defense against rot or insect damage. Select posts that are straight and free of deep cracks, large knots, or other natural defects that could compromise their strength. Try not to cut off the factory-treated ends when trimming the posts to length; they contain more of the treatment chemicals and generally last longer than cut ends. Face the factory ends down against the post hardware where water is more likely to accumulate.

Use galvanized metal post anchors to attach the posts to concrete footings. If posts are set directly on concrete, the ends won't dry properly. You'll also have a harder time making the necessary mechanical connection to the footings. Post anchors have drainage holes and pedestals that raise the ends of the wood above the footings and improve drainage. Make sure the posts are installed plumb for maximum strength.

TOOLS + MATERIALS

Pencil	Metal post anchors
Framing square	Nuts and washers for J-bolts
Ratchet wrench and sockets	Lumber for posts
Tape measure	6d galvanized common nails
Power miter saw or circular saw	2" drywall screws
Hammer	Long, straight 2 × 4, 1 × 4s
Drill/driver	Pointed 2 × 2 stakes
Level	Ear and eye protection
Speed square	Work gloves

How to Attach Post Anchors

Mark the top of each footing as a reference line for installing post anchors. Lay a long, straight 2 × 4 flat across two or three concrete footings, parallel to the ledger, with one edge tight against the J-bolts.

Draw a reference line across each concrete footing, using the edge of a 2 × 4 as a guide. Remove the 2 × 4.

Place a metal post anchor on each concrete footing, and center it over the J-bolt.

(continued)

Standoff plate

(4)

(5)

Use a framing square to make sure the post anchor is positioned square to the reference line drawn on the footing.

Thread a nut over each J-bolt, and tighten it securely with a ratchet wrench or impact driver.

 ## How to Set Posts

(1)

House

6 × 6 posts on
concrete footings

Ledger

A

POST ELEVATION

(2)

Use the elevation drawing from your design plan to find the length of each post (A). Add 6" to the length for a cutting margin.

Cut posts with a power miter saw or circular saw. Make sure factory-treated ends of posts are square. If necessary, square them by trimming with a power miter saw or circular saw.

Place the post in the anchor and tack it into place with a single 6d galvanized common nail. Do not drive the nail all the way in. If a standoff plate was provided with the post anchor hardware you are installing, position it in place before setting the post in the anchor. Some post anchors do not have supplied standoff plates, in which case you will need to drill a hole in the bottom of the post so it fits over the anchor bolt.

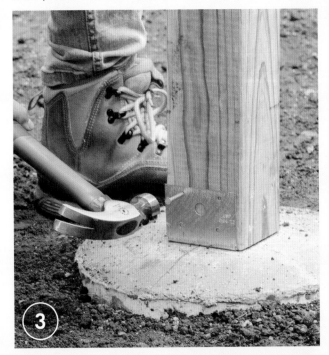

Brace the post with a 1 × 4. Place the 1 × 4 flat across the post so that it crosses the post at a 45° angle about halfway up.

Attach the brace to the post temporarily with a single 2" drywall screw.

Drive a pointed 2 × 2 stake into the ground next to the end of the brace.

(continued)

Use a level to make sure the post is plumb. Adjust the post, if necessary.

Attach the brace to the stake with two 2" drywall screws.

Plumb and brace the post on the side perpendicular to the first brace.

Attach the post to the post anchor with the fasteners specified by the hardware manufacturer. (You can also mark the post and then remove it and cut it on the ground, then nail it in place.)

Position a straight board with one end on the ledger and the other end across the face of the post. Level the board. Draw a line on the post along the bottom of the board. This line indicates the top of the joists.

TIP: Most deckbuilders recommend that the joists slope away from the house very slightly to encourage water runoff. To accomplish this, simply measure down from your mark a distance equal to ⅛" per foot of joist length.

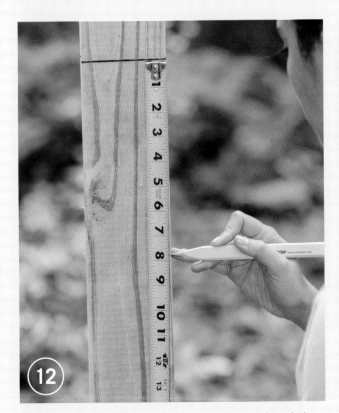

From the line shown in step 11, measure down and mark the posts a distance equal to the width of the joists.

Use a square to draw a line completely around the post. This line indicates the top of the beam. From this line, repeat steps 12 and 13 to determine the bottom of the beam.

Installing Beams

Deck beams attach to the posts to help support the weight of the joists and decking. Installation methods depend on the deck design and local codes, so check with a building inspector to determine what is acceptable in your area.

In a saddle beam deck, the beam is attached directly on top of the posts. Metal fasteners, called post saddles, are used to align and strengthen the beam-to-post connection. The advantage is that the post bears the weight of the deck.

A notched-post deck requires 6 × 6 posts notched at the post top to accommodate the full size of the beam. The deck's weight is transferred to the posts, as in a post-and-beam deck.

In years past, a third style of beam construction, called sandwiching, was also generally acceptable for deck construction. It consisted of two beams that straddled both sides of the post, connected by long through bolts. Because this method has less strength than the saddle or notched styles, it is no longer acceptable under most building codes.

TOOLS + MATERIALS

Tape measure	Reciprocating saw or handsaw
Pencil	
Circular saw	Clear sealer-preservative
Paintbrush	2½" galvanized deck screws
Speed square or combination square	10d joist hanger nails
Drill/driver and bits	Carriage bolts, washers, and nuts
Ratchet wrench and sockets or impact driver	Silicone caulk
Caulk gun	Ear and eye protection
Pressure-treated lumber	Work gloves

Deck beams, resting in a notch on the tops of the posts and secured with through bolts and nuts, guarantee strong connections that will bear the weight of your deck.

FABRICATING BEAMS

Support beams for decks usually are fabricated on site by building up two or three lengthy pieces of dimensional lumber together. The lumber, 2 × 8 or larger, should be exterior rated. Pressure-treated pine is a good choice. Some deckbuilders cut strips of ½"-thick exterior plywood to the same dimension as the beam members and sandwich the plywood between the boards. This increases the dimensional stability of the beam, making it less likely to warp or twist. It also increases the bearing strength and has the added advantage of increasing the total thickness of the beam so it fits neatly into a post saddle designed for 4× lumber (3½" actual thickness). However, plywood is not a required element in deck beams and may be left out if only for visual reasons.

To make a built-up beam, select two straight boards of the same dimension, taking particular care to avoid lumber that is twisted or crowned. Lay the boards face to face to see which alignment comes closest to flush on all sides. Apply exterior-grade construction adhesive to one board and lay the mating board onto it. Drive a pair of 10d nails near the end of the assembly to pin the boards together. Then, clamp the beam members together every 2 to 3 feet, forcing the boards into alignment as you go, if necessary. Drive 10d nails in a regular, staggered pattern every 12" to 16" or so. Flip the beam over and repeat the nailing pattern from the other side. For added strength, cross-nail the beams at about a 30° angle periodically. If the beam stock is longer than the required beam length, wait until the beam is assembled before you trim it to length. Finally, apply wood preservative to any cut end before you install the beam.

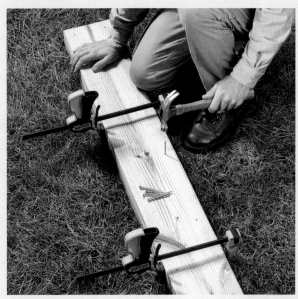

OPTIONS FOR SUPPORTING JOISTS WITH BEAMS

Beams may be installed to support the deck joists from below, or you may choose to attach joist hangers to the sides of the beams and hang the joists so the tops are flush with the beam, as seen here.

How to Make a Post/Beam Connection Using a Two-piece Cap

Fabricate the beam by face-nailing two (or three, depending on your plan) pieces of identically sized dimensional lumber. See previous page.

Measure along the beam to mark the post locations, making sure the ends of the boards of a doubled beam are flush. Mark both the near and far edges of each post onto the beam.

Use a speed square or combination square to transfer the post marks onto the top and then the opposite face of the beam, allowing you to make sure the post and post hardware align with both faces.

Cut the post to final height after securing it in place. Make two passes with a circular saw and finish with a reciprocating saw or handsaw. Take your time and try and get the cut as smooth and flat as possible.

Set both halves of the two-part post cap on top of the cut post, spread as far apart as they can go. With a helper, lower the beam into position on the post and then slide the two halves of the cap flush against the side of the beam.

Trace along the outside edge of each cap half to mark their position onto the top of the post. Remove the two-part saddle and the beam.

Replace the saddle parts onto the post, aligned with the reference marks you drew. Nail each cap half to the post by driving joist hanger nails or 8d galvanized nails through the holes in the nailing flanges. Attach caps on each post on which the beam will bear.

Replace the beam in position and secure it to the posts by driving nails through the top nailing flanges of the cap and into the beam.

How to Make a Post/Beam Connection Using a One-piece Cap

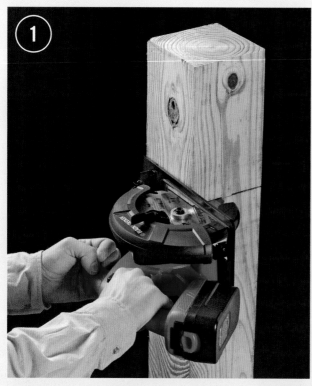

Cut the post to final height after securing it in place. Make two passes with a circular saw and finish with a reciprocating saw or handsaw.

Attach the cap hardware to the top of the post using the fasteners recommended by the manufacturer. You must drive a fastener at every predrilled hole in the cap hardware.

Set the beam into the cap, making sure the sides of the cap align with the layout marks on the beam.

Secure the beam into the cap by driving galvanized fasteners through the predrilled holes in the top half of the saddle.

How to Install a Beam for a Notched-post Deck

Remove 6 × 6 posts from post anchors and cut to finished height. Measure and mark a notch at the top of each post, sized to fit the thickness and width of the beam. Trace the lines on all sides using a framing square.

Use a circular saw to rough cut the notches, then switch to a reciprocating saw or handsaw to finish. Reattach posts to the post anchors, with the notch side facing away from the deck.

With someone's help, lift the beam (crown side up) into the notches. Align the beam and clamp it to the post. Counterbore two ½"-deep holes, using a 1⅜" spade bit, then drill ½" pilot holes through the beam and post, using a ½" auger bit.

Insert carriage bolts in to each pilot hole. Add a washer and nut to the counterbore side of each, and tighten using a ratchet. Seal both ends with silicone caulk. Apply self-sealing membrane to top surfaces of beam and posts if necessary (see page 58).

Hanging Joists

Joists provide support for the decking boards. They are attached to the ledger and header joist with galvanized metal joist hangers and are nailed or strapped to the top of the beam.

For strength and durability, use pressure-treated lumber for all joists. The exposed outside joists and header joist can be faced with composite or cedar boards for a more attractive appearance.

TOOLS + MATERIALS

Tape measure
Pencil
Hammer
Combination square
Circular saw
Paintbrush

Drill
Twist bits (⅛", ¼")
Pressure-treated lumber
10d joist hanger nails
10d and 16d galvanized
  common nails

Clear sealer-preservative
Joist angle brackets
Galvanized metal joist hangers
Ear and eye protection
Work gloves

Metal joist hangers attached to rim joists or ledgers are practically foolproof for hanging intermediate deck joists. Look for hanger hardware that is triple-dipped galvanized metal or stainless steel.

How to Hang Joists

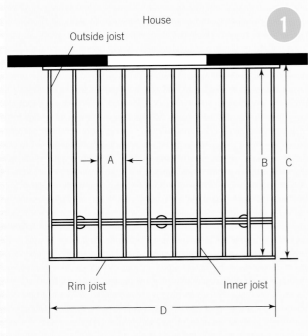

House

Outside joist

A

B

C

Rim joist

Inner joist

D

JOIST PLAN

Use your deck plan to find the spacing (A) between joists, and the length of inner joists (B), outside joists (C), and rim joist (D). Measure and mark lumber for outside joists, using a combination square as a guide. Cut joists with a miter or circular saw. Seal cut ends with clear sealer-preservative.

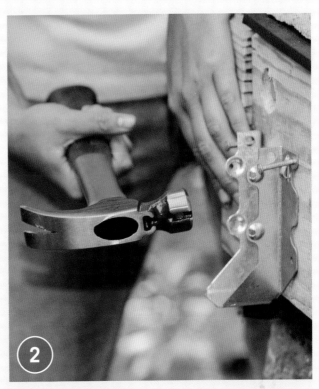

Attach joist hanger hardware near each end of the ledger board, according to your layout. Previous building codes allowed you to face nail the joists into the ends of the ledger, but this is no longer accepted practice. Attach enough fasteners only to hold the hanger in position while you square up the joist layout.

Attach the outside joists to the top of the beam by toenailing them with 10d galvanized common nails.

Trim off the ends of structural lumber to get a clean, straight edge. *(continued)*

Outside joist

Ledger

Outside joist

Beam

5

Measure and cut the outer joists, often called the rim joists. Hang them from the ledger with joist hanger hardware and either rest them on the main bearing beam and toenail them in place, or hang the other ends from joist hangers attached to the beam on the face closer to the house. Refer to your plan.

6

Finish nailing the end joist hangers, making sure you have a joist hanger nail in every punched hole in the hanger.

7

Measure along the ledger from the edge of the outside joist, and mark where the joists will be attached to the ledger.

Draw the outline of each joist on the ledger, using a square as a guide.

Measure along the beam from the outside joist, and mark where joists will cross the beam. Draw the outlines across the top of both beam boards.

Measure along the header joist from the outside joist, and mark where joists will be attached to the header joist. Draw the outlines on the inside of the header, using a square as a guide. Install the joist hangers on the rim joist.

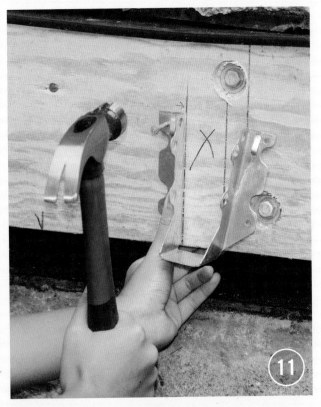

Attach joist hangers to the ledger. Position each hanger so that one of the flanges is against the joist outline. Nail one flange to framing members with fasteners specified by the manufacturer. *(continued)*

Cut a scrap board to use as a spacer. Hold the spacer inside each joist hanger, then close the hanger around the spacer.

Nail the remaining side flange to the framing member with 10d joist hanger nails. Remove the spacer.

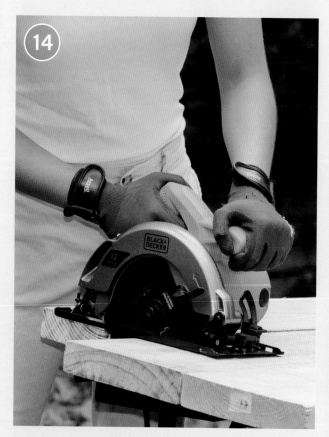

Measure and mark lumber for joists, using a combination square as a guide. Cut joists with a circular saw or power miter saw.

Seal cut ends with clear sealer-preservative. Place the joists in the hangers with crowned edge up.

Attach the ledger joist hangers to the joists with joist hanger nails. Drive nails into both sides of each joist.

Align the joists with the outlines drawn on the top of the beam. Anchor the joists to the beam by toenailing from both sides with 10d galvanized nails.

 ALTERNATE METHOD

Fasten joists to beams using H-fit joist ties for strength and durability.

OPTION: End nail the joists to reinforce the connections by driving three 10d galvanized nails through the rim joist into each inner joist. If you will not be cladding the rim joists and it will be visible, use 10d galvanized finish nails.

Decking

The decking material and installation method will help determine the joist spacing of the deck. In addition, all decking must provide a comfortable surface on which to walk. It must be strong, durable, and slip resistant. Resistance to stains, fading, and other damage is a bonus.

Although wood remains the most popular decking material, that may soon change because any homeowner can select from a variety of manufactured decking. The most notable and popular are composites and PVC decking. Composites continue to grow in popularity because they are easy to install, low maintenance, and—most importantly—come in an ever-increasing selection of colors and appearances. Composites are also available in convincing imitations of a many different woods, including hardwoods. High-end composites and PVC decking are extremely durable and long lasting, although more expensive than most woods.

Regardless of the material, you can create a more interesting look in your deck by laying decking boards in unusual patterns. Diagonals, herringbones, and other patterns are all more visually interesting than a simple linear style. Patterns do, however, entail more effort and greater expense.

In addition to the material and pattern options presented in this chapter, you'll find information on different fastener styles. These include a growing number of "invisible" fasteners that leave the surface of your deck unmarked.

In this chapter:
- Decking Patterns
- Laying Decking

Decking Patterns

Decking boards are the most visible element of your deck, and there are a number of ways to install them. You can use different board widths and lay the boards in any of a number of patterns to increase visual interest. The pattern you choose will affect joist spacing and layout. For instance, a straight decking pattern usually requires joists spaced 16 inches on-center. Diagonal decking generally requires joist spacing of 12 inches on-center. Parquet and other intricate patterns may require extra support, such as double joists or additional blocking. For sturdy wood decking, always use at least 5/4 lumber. Thinner boards are more likely to twist or cup.

Diagonal decking is one of the simplest alternatives to straight runs, and can be an interesting look—especially if you run the diagonals in different directions on different platforms or levels of the deck. However, diagonal patterns often require joists spaced closer than a straight pattern.

Parquet patterns are visually stunning and best suited to more formal decks, and those that don't include bi- or multicolored design features. These patterns require double joists and blocking to provide adequate support surface for attaching the butted ends of boards.

Double joist

Blocking

Even a straight pattern can be interesting when interrupted with built-in shapes. A framed opening for a tree or large rock requires extra blocking between joists. Short joists are attached to blocking with joist hangers.

Border patterns with mitered corners provide an elegant finished look to any deck. They are especially effective when used around the inside deck edge bordering a swimming pool. Install trim joists to support the border decking.

Laying Decking

Buy decking boards that are long enough to span the width of the deck, if possible. If you have to use more than one, butt the boards end-to-end over a joist. Stagger butted joints so that they do not overlap row to row.

Install decking so that there is a gap approximately ⅛ inch between boards to provide drainage. You can use a nail as a spacer between rows. Some wood boards naturally "cup" as they age. Lay the boards with the bark side facing down (see page 45), so that any cupping occurs on the bottom side, and to prevent the board from holding water on the top.

The common installation method for wood decking is shown here. We've limited the discussion to face-screwing boards to joists, but you can nail the boards down as well. However, nailing is rarely used on modern decking because it requires as much work, and nails inevitably pop down the road. Screws are just more efficient. If you do decide to nail boards

down, use 10d galvanized common nails, angling the nails toward each other to improve holding power. Composite and plastic deck boards are never nailed down. For a much sleeker appearance, you can choose from the large number of "invisible" fasteners on the market. The technology for these has come a long way and, whether you're using wood, composite, or another type of deck boards, hidden fasteners are an easy and quick option to screwing the boards down. In any case, always follow the installation instructions and methods recommended by the manufacturer of the product you select.

How to Lay Decking

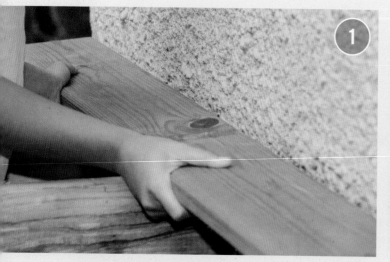

Position the first row of decking ⅛" away from the house. The first decking board should be perfectly straight, and should be precut to proper length. Attach the first decking board by driving a pair of 2½" corrosion-resistant deck screws into each joist.

Position remaining decking boards so that ends overhang outside joists. Space boards about ⅛" apart. Attach boards to each joist with a pair of 2½" deck screws driven into each joist. Avoid overdriving screws.

If the boards are bowed, use a pry bar to maneuver them into position while fastening. You can also use a specialized tool (see page 61) to align a warped board.

Drill ⅛" pilot holes in the ends of boards before attaching them to the outside joists. Pilot holes prevent screws from splitting decking boards at ends.

After every few rows of decking are installed, measure from the edge of the decking board to the edge of header joist. If the measurements show that the last board will not fit flush against the edge of the deck, adjust board spacing.

Adjust board spacing by changing the gaps between boards by a small amount over three or four rows of boards. Very small spacing changes will not be obvious to the eye.

TIP: Although 10d common nails can be used as spacers to keep gaps even, a decking spacer tool (inset) is easier to manage. *(continued)*

Use a chalk line to mark the edge of the decking flush with the outside of deck. Cut off decking using a circular saw. Set the saw blade ⅛" deeper than the thickness of the decking so that the saw will not cut the side of the deck. At areas where the circular saw cannot reach, finish the cutoff with a jigsaw or handsaw.

For a more attractive appearance, clad the exposed outside joists of the deck with fascia boards. Miter cut the corners, and attach the boards with deck screws or 8d galvanized nails. Generally, it is preferable to have the decking overlap the top edges of the fascia so you are not creating a gap where debris can collect. If you are using non-wood decking, many decking manufacturers offer non-wood fascia and trim that match the color, style, and texture of the decking.

How to Install PVC Trim Boards

In addition to wood fascia, you can also use PVC trim boards to improve the appearance of support posts, as well as rim joists. Screw 1 × 4 panels to the sides of the posts using stainless-steel trim screws. (This is a 4 × 4 post; adjust the trim panel size for larger posts.)

Rip two 1 × 6 panels down to 5" for the front and back of the posts. Secure the panels with stainless-steel trim-head screws.

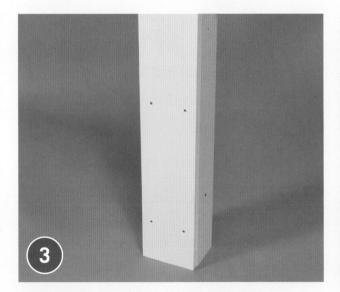

Posts finished in this way require little maintenance. An alternative to using individual panels is to use post wrap kits. These products have grooves cut into them that allow you to wrap the material around the post. They are held in place with adhesive.

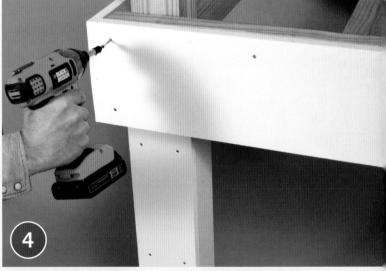

Attach rim joist cladding using 1 × 8 PVC panels. (Adjust cladding to fit rim joist dimensions if different from 2 × 8. Miter outside corners for a finished appearance. Secure using stainless-steel trim screws.

How to Conceal Fasteners in Wood Decking

1

In most cases, the fasteners you will use to attach the decking boards will remain visible. But many people like to hide the fasteners if they are using an exotic decking material by concealing the screw heads under a wood plug. Drill a hole the same width and depth as the plug.

2

Drill a pilot hole in the bottom of the plug hole you just drilled. Then drive a deck screw into the hole. The head of the screw will be below the surface of the deck.

3

Brush some exterior wood glue on the bottom and sides of the wood plugs and place them in the holes. Tap each with a rubber mallet to set them in place.

4

Part of the plug will be above the deck surface. You can remove most of the material using a sharp chisel or a belt sander. Follow with an orbital sander.

Composite + PVC Decking

Lay composite decking as you would wood decking (pages 112 to 114). Position with the factory crown up so water will run off, and space rows ⅛" to ¼" apart for drainage.

Drill pilot holes at ¾ the diameter of the fasteners, but do not countersink. Composite materials allow fasteners to set themselves. Use the fastener recommended by the manufacturer.

Cut away for clarity

ALTERNATE METHOD: Attach composite decking with self-tapping composite screws. These specially designed screws require no pilot holes. If the decking "mushrooms" over the screw head, use a hammer to tap the decking back in place.

Lay remaining decking. For boards 16' or shorter, leave a gap at deck ends and any butt joints, ¹⁄₁₆" for every 20°F difference between the temperature at the time of installation and the expected high temperature for the year.

Tongue-and-Groove Decking

Position the starter strip at the far end of the deck. Make sure it is straight and properly aligned. Attach it with 2½" galvanized deck screws driven into the lower runner found under the lip of the starter strip.

Fit the tongue of a deck board into the groove of the starter strip. There will be approximately a ¼" gap between the deck board and the starter strip. Fasten the deck board to the joists with 2½" galvanized deck screws, working from the middle out to the sides of the deck.

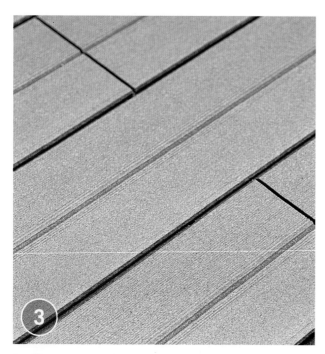

Continue to add decking. To lay deck boards end-to-end, leave a ⅛" gap between them, and make sure any butt joints are centered over a joist.

Place the final deck board and attach it with 2½" galvanized deck screws driven through the top of the deck board into the joist. If necessary, rip the final board to size, then support the board with a length of 1 × 1 and attach both to the joist. Attach facing boards to conceal exposed ends (photo 4, next page).

T-clip Decking

Insert 2" galvanized deck screws into T-clips. Loosely attach one T-clip to the ledger at each joist location.

Position a deck board tight against the T-clips. Loosely attach T-clips against bottom lip on front side of deck board, just tight enough to keep the board in place. Fully tighten T-clips at the back of the board, against the house.

Push another deck board tightly against the front T-clips, attach T-clips at the front of the new board, then fully tighten the previous set of T-clips. Add another deck board and repeat the process to the end of the deck.

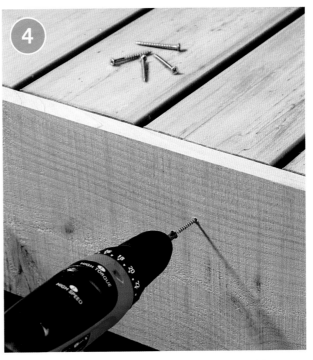

Cover exposed deck board ends. Miter cut corners of the facing, and drill pilot holes ¾ the diameter of the screws. Attach with 3" galvanized deck screws.

How to Install Decking with Spiked Clips

Drive a spiked clip into the edge of wood decking at joist locations. Use the included fastening block to prevent damage to the spikes.

Drive a deck screw through the hole in the clip and down at an angle through the deck board and into the joist. One screw secures two deck boards at each joist location.

Set the adjacent deck board into place. Tap it against the clips to seat the spikes, using a scrap block and hand maul or sledgehammer.

How to Install Decking with Biscuit-style Clips

Cut a #20 biscuit slot into the edge of deck boards at each joist location using a biscuit joiner (plate joiner). Set the slot height so the bottom edge of the biscuit clip will touch the joist edge.

Insert the biscuit clip into the slot. Drive a deck screw through the hole in the clip and down at an angle through the deck board and into the joist. One screw secures two deck boards at this joist location.

Second board

#20 biscuit slots

First board

Lay a bead of construction adhesive along the edge of the joist to keep it from squeaking later. Cut slots in the adjacent deck board and fit it over the clips of the previous board.

THE CASE FOR HIDDEN FASTENERS

The hidden fastener options shown here are only a few of the excellent alternatives to conventional face-nailing or screwing methods. The biggest advantage is aesthetic: no screwheads or nail heads mar the surface of your deck. But there are other benefits to hidden fasteners as well. Face-screwed wood decking is more prone to rotting, because water can collect in the screw head pockets. If you nail the decking down, the nail heads are bound to eventually pop up as the decking dries, contracts, or moves under use and wear. Hidden fasteners eliminate both of these problems. If you use spike- or biscuit-style clip systems, be aware that you may need to remove large sections of deck boards in order to replace a damaged or defective board in the future, because the fasteners lock adjacent boards together and hide access to the fasteners. The same is true of many other hidden-fastener systems.

How to Install Decking with Undermount Deck Brackets

Install the deck brackets along the top edge of each joist, alternating brackets from one side of the joist to the other in a continuous series. Secure the brackets with screws driven into the side of the joist.

Secure the deck boards by driving screws up through the bracket holes and into the joists. Depending on space constraints, these screws can be driven from above if necessary.

Continue installing all of the deck boards from below. When you reach the last board, you may need to install it from above for access reasons. Drive deck screws through the deck board and into the joists below. To maintain the hidden fastener appearance, counterbore the pilot holes for the screws and fill the counterbore with a plug cut from a piece of scrap decking.

How to Install Decking with Undermount Clips

Set a deck board into place on the joists, and slide a clip against it so the spacer tab touches the edge of the deck board. Drive a screw through the center hole of the clip and into the joist.

Drive a deck screw up through the plastic clip and into the deck board to secure it.

Position the next deck board against the clip's spacer tab, and drive a deck screw up through the clip to fasten it in place. One clip secures two deck boards at each joist location.

Stairs

Nearly every deck, including most low-profile decks, requires at least one step to reach the deck platform. For complex, multilevel decks or decks built on steep slopes, you may need to build several runs of stairs and possibly even a landing. Given the potential risks when using deck stairs, the International Residential Code is very specific regarding the size and spacing of treads and risers, the minimum stair width, and the structural sizes for stringers. Here's where your local building official can help you steer clear of potential code violations so you can build a safe stair system that will pass inspection.

Because the vertical drop of every deck varies, you'll need to make several calculations to figure out exactly what the layout of your stairs will be. This chapter will show you how. You'll also learn basic stair construction, how to build a longer flight of stairs with a landing, and even how to build a simple box-frame or suspended step when your deck is close to the ground.

In this chapter:
- Stairway Styles
- How to Build a Box-frame Step
- How to Build a Suspended Step
- How to Make Stair Stringers
- How to Build Basic Deck Stairs

Building Stairs

How you build stairs and railings for your deck is perhaps the most tightly regulated portion of the building code related to decks. Whenever you are in doubt about measurements for deck stairs—or wondering if you even need to install stairs in the first place—consult the local building codes or local building inspector. Basically, designing deck stairs involves four calculations:

The number of stairs depends on the vertical drop of the deck—the distance from the deck surface to the nearest ground level.

Rise is the vertical space between treads. The proper rise prevents stumbling on the stairs. Most codes call for a maximum rise of 7¾ inches while a lower rise generally makes it easier to ascend or descend the stairs. The thickness of one tread is added to the space between steps to determine actual rise.

Run is the depth of the treads, and is usually a minimum of 10 inches, although the deeper the tread, the more comfortable the stairs will be. Stair step thickness is also dictated by code and is usually a minimum of 1 inch, although most builders use 2× lumber for stair steps. A convenient way to build step treads is by using two 2 × 6s.

Span is calculated by multiplying the run by the number of treads. The span helps you locate the end of the stairway so that you can properly position the posts.

Specifications for other elements, such as the stringers and the method of attachment used to connect stairs to decking, are also usually mandated in local codes. For instance, stringers normally have to be at least 1½ inches thick.

Although there are different ways to construct stairs, the same basic code requirements apply to any staircase used with a deck.

TOOLS + MATERIALS

Tape measure	Drill	2 × 12 lumber	Stair treads (5/4 × 6 or 2 × 6)
Pencil	⅛" twist bit	Metal cleats	16d galvanized common nails
Framing square	1⅜" spade bit	¼" × 1¼" lag screws	Silicone caulk
Level	Ratchet wrench	Joist angle brackets	Long, straight 2 × 4
Plumb bob	Caulk gun	10d joist hanger nails	Pointed stakes
Clamshell posthole digger	Sand	½ × 4" lag screws and 1⅜" washers	Masking tape
Wheelbarrow	Portland cement		Ear and eye protection
Hoe	Gravel	2 × 6 lumber	Work gloves
Circular saw	J-bolts	3" deck screws	
Hammer	Metal post anchors	½" × 6" through bolts	

Stairway Styles

Platform steps feature wide treads. Each step is built on a framework of posts and joists.

Open steps have metal cleats, sometimes called tread angles, that hold the treads between the stringers. The treads on this stairway are built with 2 × 6s to match the surface decking.

Boxed steps, built with notched stringers and solid risers, give a finished look to a deck stairway. Predrill the ends of treads to prevent splitting.

Long stairways sometimes require landings. A landing is a small platform to which both flights of stairs are attached.

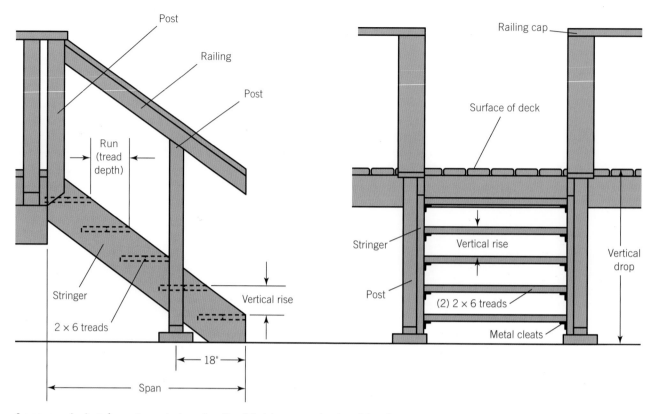

SIDE STAIR ELEVATION

Post

Railing

Post

Run
(tread
depth)

Stringer

2 × 6 treads

Vertical rise

18"

Span

FRONT STAIR ELEVATION

Railing cap

Surface of deck

Stringer

Vertical rise

Post

(2) 2 × 6 treads

Metal cleats

Vertical
drop

A common deck stairway is made from two 2 × 12 stringers and pairs of 2 × 6 treads attached with metal cleats. Posts set 18" back from the end of the stairway help to anchor the stringers and the railings. Calculations needed to build stairs include the number of steps, the rise of each step, the run of each step, and the stairway span.

HOW TO FIND MEASUREMENTS FOR STAIRWAY LAYOUT

			EXAMPLE (39" High Deck)
1. Find the number of steps: Measure vertical drop from deck surface to ground. Divide by 7. Round off to nearest whole number.	Vertical drop: ÷ 7 = Number of steps: =		39" ÷ 5.57" = 6
2. Find step rise: Divide the vertical drop by the number of steps.	Vertical drop: = Number of steps: ÷ Rise: =		39" ÷ 6 = 6.5"
3. Find step run: Typical treads made from two 2 × 6s have a run of 11¼". If your design is different, find run by measuring depth of tread, including any space between boards.	Run:		11¼"
4. Find stairway span: Multiply the run by the number of treads. (Number of treads is always one less than number of steps.)	Run: Number of treads: Span: =		11¼" × 5 = 56¼"

Simple Stairs: How to Build a Box-frame Step

Construct a rectangular frame for the step using dimension lumber (2 × 6 lumber is standard). Join the pieces with deck screws. The step must be at least 36" wide and 10" deep. Cut cross blocks and install them inside the frame, spaced every 16".

Dig a flat-bottomed trench, about 4" deep, where the step will rest. Fill the trench with compactible gravel, and pack with a tamper (some codes require a concrete footing—check with your building department). Set the step in position, then measure and attach deck boards to form the tread of the step.

 # Simple Stairs: How to Build a Suspended Step

Screw 2 × 4 furring strips against one side of the deck joists where the step joists will be installed. These strips provide an offset so the step joists will not conflict with the joist hangers attached to the beam. Use a reciprocating saw and chisel to make 1½"-wide notches in the rim joist adjacent to the furring strips.

Measure and cut step joists, allowing about 3' of nailing surface inside the deck frame, and 10" or more of exposed tread. Make sure the step joists are level with one another, then attach them to the deck joists, using deck screws. Cut and attach deck boards to the tread area of the step.

NOTE: To maintain adequate structural strength, notches in the joists should be no more than 1½" deep in a 2 × 10 beam.

How to Make Stair Stringers

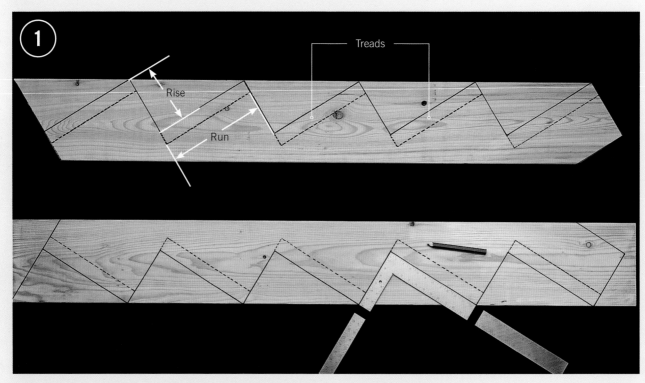

Lay out the stair stringers. Use tape to mark the rise measurement on one leg of a framing square, and the run measurement on the other leg. Beginning at one end of the stringer, position the square with tape marks flush to edge of the board, and outline the rise and run for each step. Then draw in the tread outline against the bottom of each run line. Use a circular saw to trim the ends of the stringers as shown. (When cutting the stringers for stairs without metal cleats, just cut on the solid lines.)

Attach metal tread cleats flush with the bottom of each tread outline, using fasteners specified by the manufacturer. Drill ⅛" pilot holes to prevent the screws from splitting the wood.

Hang the stringers from the rim joist of your deck with concealed stringer hanger hardware attached with 10d joist hanger nail.

Other Options for Stair Stringers

Notched stringers precut from pressure-treated wood are available at building centers. Edges of cutout areas should be coated with sealer-preservative to prevent rot.

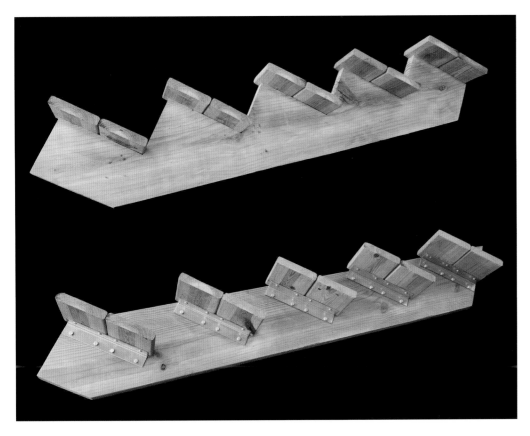

Cut your own open stringers from 2 × 12 treated lumber (top). Use a carpenter's square to lay out the treads and risers. The technique is very similar to the process shown for marking tread brace location on the previous page. You can also attach tread cleats to a solid wood stringer (bottom) for a stronger undercarriage than you'll get using open stringers. You can use strips of angle iron similar to the ones seen on the previous page, or you can opt for heavy-duty, galvanized stair treads attached with joist hanger screws, as in this photo.

How to Build Basic Deck Stairs

Use the stairway elevation drawings to confirm your design, including the locations of the stair stringers and posts. Use a pencil and framing square to outline where stair stringers will be attached to the side of the deck.

Locate the post footings according to your plan. Lay a straight 2 × 4 on the deck so that it is level and square to the side of the deck. Measure out along the 2 × 4 and use a plumb bob or level to mark the ground at footing centerpoints.

Dig holes and pour the footings for posts. Attach metal post anchors to the footings and install the posts. Check with your building department to find out if 6 × 6 posts are now required. See pages 78 to 89 for more information on locating and pouring footings.

Attach the stair stringers to the deck joist that supports them, using skewable joist hangers designed for use with stair stringers. Here, a prefabricated four-step stringer cut from pressure-treated pine is shown.

5

Attach the bottoms of the stringer to the stair railing posts using ½"-dia. through bolts with washers. Tack the post to the stringers with screws to hold it in place while you work.

6

Attach a 2 × 4 brace to the bottom ends of the stringers to help prevent racking. You'll need to trim 1½" from the bottom end of any intermediate stringers so the ends of the brace will butt against the inside faces of the outer stringers. Measure from the outside edges of the outer stringers to find the required tread length. Add an inch of overhang to each end if you wish.

7

Begin positioning the treads on the stringers, starting at the top. Two 5/4 × 6" decking boards or two 2 × 6 boards are just the right width to create a stair tread. The top of the tread on the top step should be flush with the decking.

8

Attach the stair treads with 3" deck screws. Especially when working on the outer stringers where the screws are near the ends of the board you should drill pilot holes for the screws.

9

Finish installing the treads, using a spacer such as a 10d common nail to maintain the space between tread boards. If your staircase has more than three steps, you're required to install a railing with a graspable handrail.

Deck Railings

Decks that are built 30 inches above the ground or higher must have a system of railings installed around their perimeter. Building codes dictate the important spacing and height requirements for railings, as well as how the guard rails, the posts that support the railing system, must be attached to the deck. Granted, traditional wooden railings are quick to build and relatively affordable, but there are other exciting and attractive alternatives. This chapter will show you a variety of different railing systems, including those made with prefabricated composite parts, steel cable, and even clear glass panels. With a measure of creativity on your part, railings can be a showcase design feature of your new deck and not just a means of preventing injuries.

This chapter will highlight important codes that pertain to guard rails. This chapter will also teach you how to outfit your deck stairs with handrails and balusters and even shape a curved railing using several challenging woodworking techniques.

In this chapter:
- Deck Railing Basics
- Curved Railings
- Composite + PVC Railing Systems
- Glass-panel Railings
- Steel Cable Railings

Deck Railing Basics

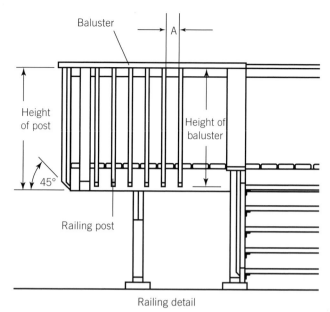

Railings must be sturdy and firmly attached to the framing members of the deck. Never attach railing posts to the surface decking. Check local building codes for guidelines regarding railing construction. Most codes require that railings be at least 36 inches above decking. Vertical balusters should be spaced no more than 4 inches apart. In some areas, a grippable handrail may be required for any stairway over four treads. Check with your local building inspector for the building codes in your area.

Railing detail

Refer to your deck design plan for spacing (A) and length of railing posts and balusters. Balusters should be placed so that there is no more than a 4" gap between adjacent balusters. Posts should be spaced no more than 6' apart.

TOOLS + MATERIALS

Tape measure	Ratchet wrench	Railing lumber (4 × 4s, 2 × 6s, 2 × 4s, 2 × 2s)	2½" corrosion-resistant deck screws
Pencil	Caulk gun	Blocking lumber (2 × blocking and 4 × 4s)	10d galvanized common nails
Power miter saw	Reciprocating saw	Clear sealer-preservative	5" and 8" structural screws
Drill	Circular saw	⅜ × 6" through bolts, nuts, and washers	Eye and ear protection
Twist bits (1/16", ⅛", ⅜")	Jigsaw with wood-cutting blade	Silicone caulk	Work gloves
1⅜" spade bit	Miter saw		
Combination square	Level		
Awl			

Railings are mandatory safety features for any deck that's more than 30" above grade. There are numerous code issues and stipulations that will dictate how you build your deck railings. Consult with your local building inspector for any code clarification you may need.

Types of Railings

Vertical balusters are a traditional look, well suited to a range of home and deck styles, and the most common type of railing construction used on decks. The balusters can be made of wood, metal, or composite.

Horizontal railings are often used on low, ranch-style homes. Horizontal railings are made of vertical posts, two or more wide horizontal rails, and a railing cap. There should be no more than 4" between the horizontal railings.

NOTE: Horizontal railings are climbable and are potentially hazardous for young children.

 RAILING CODES

Railings are required by building codes on any deck that is 30" above existing grade, although they are handy even on lower decks. Many codes are especially stringent when it comes to the fabrication of guard rails. The style of railing is, however, not mandated by code. You can choose from among the many railing styles to match the architectural style of your home, or—as is more commonly done—pick a railing style that complements the deck itself. Wood railings can be fabricated in many different styles; composite railings are usually matched in both color and detailing to the deck color and style. Synthetic railings even can be formed into complex curving shapes as necessary. Codes may require that you add easily gripped handrails on stairs with more than four risers. Always check with your local building department to ensure compliance with local codes.

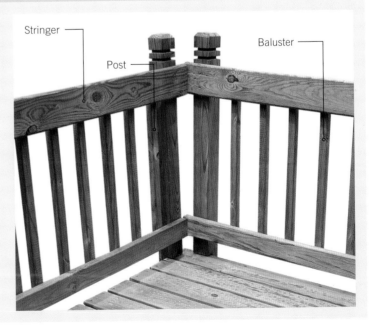

Stringer

Post

Baluster

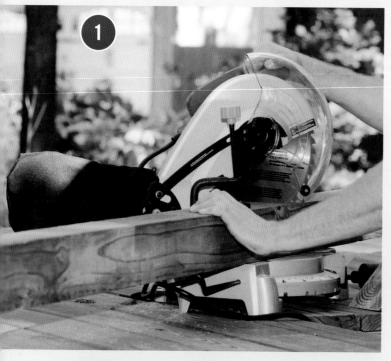

Measure and cut 4 × 4 posts using a power miter saw or circular saw. Cut the tops of the posts square, and cut the bottoms at a 45° angle. Seal cut ends of lumber with clear sealer-preservative.

Measure and cut the balusters for the main deck railing using a power miter saw or circular saw. Cut the tops of the balusters square, and cut the bottoms at a 45° angle. Seal cut ends of lumber with clear sealer-preservative.

Prepare the posts for attachment by drilling guide holes for lag bolts at the bottom of the posts. A 4 × 4 post is thick enough that you may drill shallow counterbores so the bolt head is recessed, but you'll get maximum holding power by using a lag bolt with a washer and nut on the other side of the rim joist to which the post is attached.

Drill two pilot holes spaced 4" apart near the bottom end of each baluster. Drill two pilot holes at the top of each baluster, spaced 1½" apart.

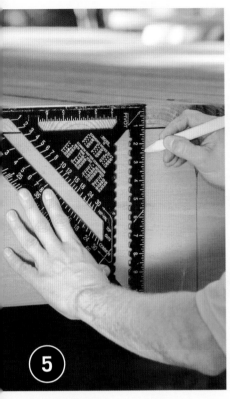

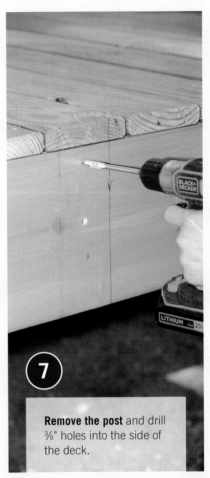

5 **Measure and mark** the position of posts around the outside of the deck using a combination square as a guide. Plan to install a post on the outside edge of each stair stringer.

6 **Position each post** with the beveled end flush with the bottom of the deck. Plumb the post with a level. Insert a screwdriver or the ⅜" drill bit into the pilot holes and mark the side of the deck.

7 **Remove the post** and drill ⅜" holes into the side of the deck.

8 **Attach railing posts** to the side of the deck with through bolts and washers. Seal the screw heads with silicone caulk if you drilled counterbores. See page 146 for different guard rail attachment techniques.

9 **Measure and cut 2 × 4 side rails.** Position the rails with their edges flush to the tops of the posts, and attach them to the posts with 2½" corrosion-resistant deck screws. *(continued)*

Join 2 × 4s for long rails by cutting the ends at 45° angles. Drill ⅛" pilot holes to prevent nails from splitting the end grain, and attach the rails with 10d galvanized nails. (Screws may split mitered ends.)

Attach the ends of rails to the stairway posts, flush with the edges of the posts, as shown. Drill ⅛" pilot holes, and attach the rails with 2½" corrosion-resistant deck screws.

At stairways, measure from the surface of the decking to the top of the upper stairway post (A).

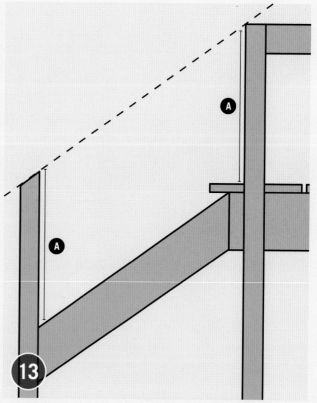

Transfer measurement A to the lower stairway post, measuring from the edge of the top of the stair stringer to the point where it meets the post.

Rail parallel

14

Position a 2 × 4 rail against the insides of the stairway posts. Align the rail with the top rear corner of the top post and with the pencil mark on the lower post. Have a helper attach the rail temporarily with 2½" deck screws.

Mark the outline of the post and the deck rail on the back side of the stairway rail.

15

Stair rail

Deck rail

16

Mark the outline of the stairway rail on the lower stairway post. Posts should be no more than 6 ft. apart.

17

Mark a plumb cutoff line at the bottom end of the stairway rail. Remove the rail. *(continued)*

Extend the pencil lines across both sides of the stairway post using a combination square as a guide and straightedge.

Cut off the lower stairway post along the diagonal cutoff line using a reciprocating saw or circular saw.

Use a circular saw or power miter saw to cut the stairway rail along the marked outlines.

Position the stairway rail flush against the top edge of the posts. Drill ⅛" pilot holes, then attach the rail to the posts with 2½" deck screws.

Use a spacer block to ensure equal spacing between balusters. Beginning next to a plumb railing post, position each baluster tight against the spacer block, with the top of the baluster flush to the top of rail. Attach each baluster with 2½" deck screws.

For the stairway guard rails, position the baluster against the stringer and rail, and adjust for plumb. Draw a diagonal cutoff line on top of the baluster, using the top of the stair rail. Cut the baluster on the marked line. Seal the ends with clear sealer-preservative.

Beginning next to the upper stairway post, position each baluster tight against the spacer block, with the top flush to the top of the stair rail. Predrill and attach the baluster with 2½" deck screws.

Position the 2 × 6 cap so that the edge is flush with the rail's inside edge. Drill ⅛" pilot holes and attach the cap to the rail with 2½" deck screws every 12". Drive screws into each post and into every third baluster. For long caps, bevel the ends at 45°. Drill 1/16" pilot holes and nail to the post with 10d nails. *(continued)*

At the corners, miter the ends of the railing cap at 45°. Drill ⅛" pilot holes, and attach the cap to the post with 2½" deck screws.

At the top of the stairs, cut the cap so that it is flush with the stairway rail. Drill ⅛" pilot holes and attach the cap with 2½" deck screws.

Measure and cut the cap for the stairway rail. Mark the outline of the post on the side of the cap, and bevel cut the ends of the cap. Position the cap over the stairway rail and balusters so that the edge of the cap is flush with the inside edge of the rail.

Drill ⅛" pilot holes and attach the cap to the rail with 2½" deck screws driven every 12". Also drive screws through the cap into the stair post and into every third baluster. If your staircase has 4 or more steps, add a graspable hand rail (see page 153).

Wood Railing Style Variations

Vertical baluster railings are a popular style because they complement most house styles. To improve the strength and appearance of the railing, the advanced variation shown here uses a "false mortise" design. The 2 × 2 balusters are mounted on 2 × 2 horizontal rails that slide into mortises notched into the posts (see page 148).

Horizontal railing best visually complements ranch-style or modern houses with predominantly horizontal lines. For improved strength and a more attractive appearance, the style shown here features 1 × 4 rails set on edge into dadoes cut in the faces of the posts. A cap rail running over all posts and top rails helps unify and strengthen the railing (see page 149).

Wall-style railing is framed with short 2 × 4 stud walls attached flush with the edges of the deck. The stud walls and rim joists are then covered with siding materials, usually chosen to match the siding on the house. A wall-style railing creates a more private space and visually draws the deck into the home, providing a unified appearance (see page 150).

Stairway railings are required for any stairway with more than three steps. They are usually designed to match the style used on the deck railing (see page 152).

Building codes have focused on the connections between guard rails, the posts that support a deck's railing system, and the rest of the deck. The practice of simply bolting a post to a rim joist does not provide the required stability necessary for guard rails. In other words, the guard rail could fail if enough force pushes it outward.

To make guard rail posts more stable, construction techniques tie the guard rail into the framing of the deck, not just the rim joist. These pages show the use of some possible techniques. They include using metal brackets, or tension ties, as well as blocking and using structural screws to provide solid guard rail-to-deck connections.

HOW TO SECURE GUARD RAILS WITH METAL BRACKETS

When installing a guard rail on the outside of the deck, follow steps 5 through 7 on page 139 for lining up the guard rail and the bracket. Attach the bracket to the deck joist. Follow the manufacturer's directions on the type of screws to use. Screws and brackets are often sold as a set.

Install through bolts with nuts and washers. The top bolt will go through the hole in the bracket. The bottom bolt that goes through only the guard rail provides added holding power.

The guard rail is securely tied into the structure of the deck because it is supported by both the rim joist and the floor joist. For situations where the guard rail falls between joists, attach brackets to the two joists that flank the position of the guard rail and use two through bolts to secure the guard rail to the rim joist.

Attach 2 × blocking to the side of the joist if the guard rail will be installed inside the rim joist. The blocking should butt up against the post. Attach the bracket and through bolts and washers as described above.

NOTE: Two possible scenarios are shown here. There are other possible techniques depending on where the guard rails fall along the perimeter of the deck.

HOW TO SECURE GUARD RAILS WITH WOOD BLOCKING

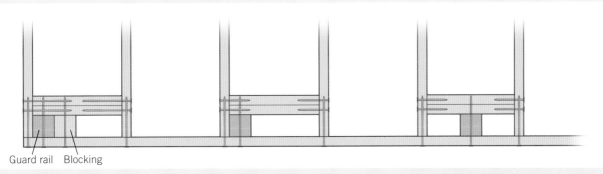

Guard rail   Blocking

Here are three possible scenarios when installing guard rails inside the rim joist. Each guard rail is reinforced by blocking and secured with structural screws rather than through bolts.

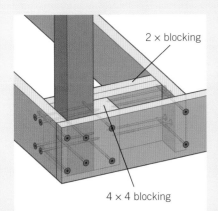

2 × blocking

4 × 4 blocking

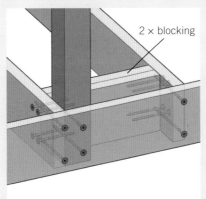

2 × blocking

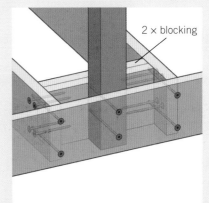

2 × blocking

Install double 2 × blocking and 4 × 4 blocking to secure a guard rail in a corner. The combination of blocking resists force in two directions. Use 8" structural screws for all connections. Be sure to offset the screws that may cross by ½". Note that screws also reinforce the connection between the rim joist, the end joist, and the first inboard floor joist.

Install double 2 × blocking to secure a guard rail that is next to an inboard joist. Use 5" screws to attach the blocking to the joist but 8" screws for other connections, including the rim joist-to-floor joist connections.

When the guard rail falls between joists, use blocking to prevent outward movement of the guard rail. Use 8" screws for connections through the rim joist and 5" screws to hold the blocking in place. Be sure to offset screws where necessary.

Install single 2 × blocking on both sides of a guard rail that falls midspan along the side rim joist. Use two 8" screws through each end of the blocking.

Install 4 × 4 blocking to support the guard rail. Drive 5" screws through the 2 × blocking into the post and the 4 × 4, two screws for each piece from both sides. Drive two 8" screws through the side rim joist into the guard rail and blocking.

How to Build a Vertical Baluster Railing

Cut 4 × 4 railing posts to size (at least 36", plus the height of the deck rim joists). Lay out and mark partial dadoes 1½" wide and 2½" long where the horizontal 2 × 2 rails will fit. Use a circular saw set to ½" blade depth to make a series of cuts from the edge of the post to the end of layout marks, then use a chisel to clean out the dadoes and square them off. On corner posts, cut dadoes on adjoining sides of the post.

Attach the posts inside the rim joists. To find the length for the rails, measure between the bases of the posts, then add 1" for the ½" dadoes on each post. Measure and cut all balusters. Install the surface boards before continuing with railing construction.

Assemble the rails and balusters on a flat surface. Position the balusters at regular intervals (no more than 4" apart), and secure them by driving 2½" deck screws through the rails. A spacing block cut to match the desired gap can make this easier.

Slide the assembled railings into the post dadoes, and toenail them in position with galvanized casing nails. Cut plugs to fit the exposed dadoes, and glue them in place. The resulting joint should resemble a mortise and tenon.

Measure and cut the 2 × 6 cap rails, then secure them by driving 2" deck screws up through the top rail. At corners, miter-cut the cap rails to form miter joints.

How to Build a Notched Deck Railing

Cut all 4 × 4 posts to length, then clamp them together to lay out 3½"-wide × ¾"-deep dadoes for the horizontal rails. For corner posts, cut dadoes on adjacent faces of the post. Cut the dadoes by making a series of parallel cuts, about ¼" apart, between the layout marks.

Knock out the waste wood between the layout marks using a hammer, then use a chisel to smooth the bottom of each dado. Attach the posts inside the rim joists. Install the decking before continuing with the railing construction.

Determine the length of the 1 × 4 rails by measuring between the bases of the posts. Cut rails to length, then nail them in place using 8d splitless siding nails or deck screws. At the corners, bevel-cut the ends of the rails to form miter joints. If any rails butt together, the joint should fall at the center of a post.

Cleat

Measure and cut 2 × 2 cleats and attach them between the posts, flush with the top rail, using galvanized casing nails. Then, measure and cut cap rails, and position and attach them by driving 2" deck screws up through the cleats. At corners, miter-cut the ends of the cap rails.

How to Build a Sided Railing

Build a 2 × 4 stud wall to match the planned height of your railing. Space studs 16" on center, and attach them by driving deck screws through the top plate and sole plate. Stud walls should be installed between properly secured posts with no wall section more than 6 ft. long.

Position the stud wall on the deck, flush with the edges of the rim joists, then anchor it by driving 3" deck screws down through the sole plate. At corners, screw the studs of adjoining walls together. At open ends, screw the end studs to posts.

At corners, attach 2 × 4 nailers flush with the inside and outside edges of the top plate and sole plate to provide a nailing surface for attaching trim boards and siding materials.

On inside corners, attach a 2 × 2 trim strip using 10d splitless cedar siding nails. Siding materials will be butted against this trim strip.

On outside corners, attach a 1×3, then overlap it with a 1×4 so the sides look equal. The trim boards should extend down over the rim joist. Also attach trim boards around posts.

Cut and position cap rails on the top rail, then secure them with 2" deck screws driven up through the rail. Railing caps should be mitered at the corners.

Attach siding materials to the inside and outside faces of the wall, using splitless cedar siding nails. Snap level chalk lines for reference, and try to match the reveal used on your house siding; the first course should overhang the rim joist slightly. Where joints are necessary, stagger them from course to course so they do not fall on the same studs.

How to Build an Angled Stair Railing

Use a combination square to mark the face of the top stairway post, where the railings will fit. For most horizontal stairway designs, the top stairway rail should start level with the second deck rail. Mark the other stairway posts at the same level.

Position a rail board against the faces of the posts, with the bottom edge against the stringer, then scribe angled cutting lines across the rail along the inside edges of the posts. Cut the rail at these lines, then cut the remaining rails to match.

Secure the rails to the posts with galvanized metal L-brackets attached to the insides of the rails.

Measure and cut a 2 × 2 cleat, and attach it flush with the top inside edge of the top rail, using 2" deck screws. Anchor the cleat to the posts by toenailing with galvanized casing nails.

Measure and cut the cap rail to fit over the top rail and cleat. At the bottom of the railing, cut the post at an angle and attach the cap rail so it overhangs the post slightly. Secure the cap rail by driving 2" deck screws up through the cleat.

Measure and cut a grippable handrail, attaching it to the posts with mounting brackets. Miter cut the ends, and create a return back to the post by cutting another mitered section of handrail and nailing it in place between the handrail and post (right).

GRIPPABLE HANDRAILS

Grippable handrails are required for stairways with 4 risers or more. The handrail should be shaped so the grippable portion is between 1¼" and 2" in diameter, and should be angled into posts at the ends. The top of the handrail should be 34" to 38" above the stair treads, measured from the nose of a step.

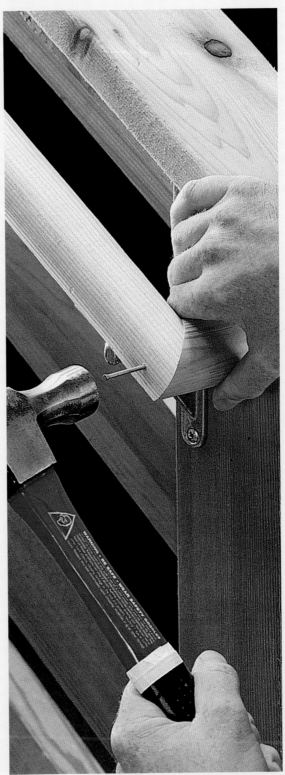

Curved Railings

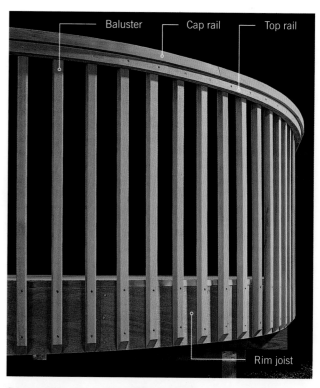

Laying out and constructing a curved railing requires a basic understanding of geometry and the ability to make detailed drawings using a compass, protractor, and a special measuring tool called a scale ruler. It is a fairly advanced technique, but the results are worth the effort. Making the top rail involves bending and gluing thinner strips of wood together around the deck's curved rim joist, which acts like a bending form. You'll need lots of medium-sized clamps on hand to hold the railing in the proper shape while it dries. The cap rail is formed by joining several mitered pieces of lumber together, end to end, to form an oversized blank, then cutting out the curved shape.

The method for constructing a curved cap rail shown on the following pages works only for symmetrical curves—quarter circles, half circles, or full circles. If your deck has irregular or elliptical curves, creating a cap rail is very difficult. For these curves, it is best to limit the railing design to include only balusters and a laminated top rail. Lastly, if this seems too complicated for your skills, you can opt for a composite curved railing, which can be made to order.

Components of a curved railing include: vertical balusters attached to the curved rim joist, a top rail built from laminated layers of plywood, and a curved cap rail. The cap rail is constructed by laying out mitered sections of 2 × 12 lumber, marking a curved shape, and cutting it out with a jigsaw.

A curved cap rail is created from mitered segments of 2 × 12 lumber. After positioning the 2 × 12 segments end to end, the shape of the 6"-wide cap rail is outlined on the pieces. For a semicircle with a radius of up to 7', four 2 × 12 segments will be needed, with ends mitered at 22½°. For a semicircle with a larger radius, you will need eight segments, with ends mitered at 11¼°.

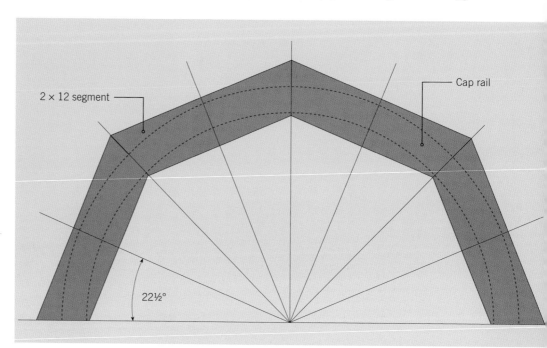

How to Build a Curved Railing

To create a curved top rail, use exterior glue to laminate four 1½"-wide strips of ⅜"-thick cedar plywood together, using the curved rim joist of the deck as a bending form. (To create curved rim joists, see page 186.) First, cover the rim joist with kraft paper for protection. Then, begin wrapping strips of plywood around the rim joist. Clamp each strip in position, starting at one end of the curve. The strips should differ in length to ensure that butt joints will be staggered from layer to layer.

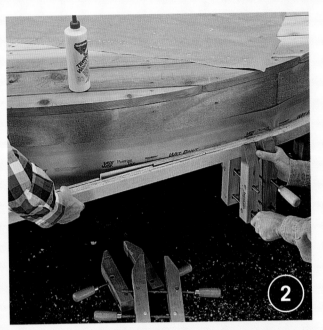

Continue working your way around the rim joist, toward the other end. Make sure to apply clamps on both sides of the butt joints where plywood strips meet. Cut the last strips slightly long, then trim the laminated rail to the correct length after the glue has set. For extra strength, drive 1" deck screws through the rail at 12" intervals after all strips are glued together. Unclamp the rail, and sand the top and bottom edges smooth.

Install posts at the square corners of the deck. Then, cut 2 × 2 balusters to length, beveling the bottom ends at 45°. Attach the balusters to the rim joist with 2½" deck screws, using a spacer to maintain even intervals. Clamp the curved top rail to the tops of the balusters and posts, then attach it with deck screws.

After the top rail and balusters are in place, attach 2 × 2 top rails to the balusters in the straight sections of the deck. The ends of the straight top rails should be flush against the ends of the curved top rail. Now, measure the distance between the inside faces of the balusters at each end of the curve. Divide this distance in half to find the required radius for the curved cap rail. *(continued)*

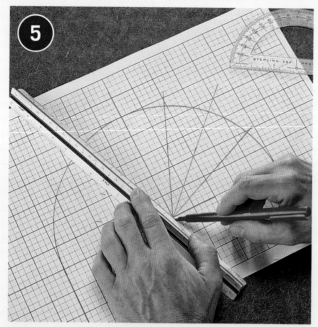

Using a scale of 1" to 1', make a diagram of the deck. (A scale ruler makes this job easier.) First, draw the arc of the deck with a compass, using the radius measurement found in step 4. Divide the curved portion of the deck into an even number of equal sections by using a protractor to draw radius lines from the center of the curve. For a semicircular curve, it is usually sufficient to draw eight radius lines, angled at 22½° to one another. (For a deck with a radius of more than 7', you may need to divide the semicircle into 16 portions, with radius lines angled at 11¼°.)

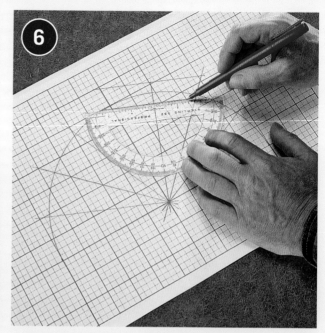

From the point where one of the radius lines intersects the curved outline of the deck, use the scale ruler to mark points 5½" above and 5½" below the intersection. From these points, use a protractor to draw perpendicular lines to the adjoining radius lines. The polygon outlined by the perpendicular lines and the adjoining radius lines represents the shape and size for all of the 2 × 12 segments that will be used to construct the cap rail.

Draw a pair of parallel arcs 5½" apart, representing the curved cap railing, inside the outline for the 2 × 12 segments. Shade the portion of the drawing that lies between the straight parallel lines and the two adjacent radius lines. This area represents the shape and size for each of the angled 2 × 12 segments. Measure the angle of the miter at the ends of the board; in this example, the segments are mitered at 22½°.

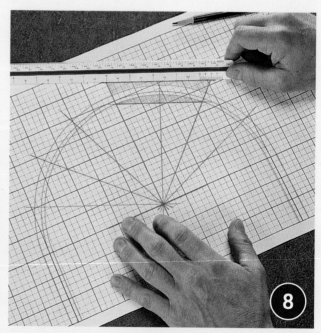

Measure the length of the long edge; this number is the overall length for each of the 2 × 12 segments you will be cutting. Using this highlighted area, determine how many segments you will need to complete the curve. For a semicircular curve with a radius of up to 7', four segments are required, with ends mitered at 22½°. For curves with a larger radius, you need eight segments, with ends mitered at 11¼°.

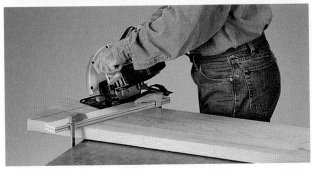

Measure and mark 2 × 12 lumber for the cap rail segments, with ends angled inward at 22½° from perpendicular. Set the blade on your circular saw or tablesaw to a 15° bevel, then make compound miter cuts along the marked lines. When cut to compound miters, the segments will form overlapping scarf joints that are less likely to reveal gaps between the boards.

Arrange the cap rail segments over the curved deck railing, and adjust the pieces, if necessary, so they are centered over the top rail. When you are satisfied with the layout, temporarily attach the segments in place by driving 2" deck screws up through the curved top rail. Measure and install the 2 × 6 cap railing for the straight portion of the railing.

Temporarily nail or clamp a long sturdy board between the sides at the start of the curve. Build a long compass, called a trammel, by nailing one end of a long 1 × 2 to a 1'-long piece of 1 × 4. Measure from the nail out along the arm of the trammel, and drill holes at the desired radius measurements; for our application, there will be two holes, 5½" apart, representing the width of the finished cap rail. Attach the 1 × 4 base of the trammel to the temporary board so the nail point is at the centerpoint of the deck rail curve, then insert a pencil through one of the holes in the trammel arm. Pivot the arm of the trammel around the cap rail, scribing a cutting line. Move the pencil to the other hole, and scribe a second line.

Remove the trammel and unscrew the cap rail segments. Use a jigsaw to cut along the scribed lines, then reposition the curved cap rail pieces over the top rail. Secure the cap rail by applying exterior adhesive to the joints and driving 2½" deck screws up through the top rail. Use a belt sander to remove saw marks.

Even if you are committed to using wood posts and railings for your deck, there are numerous ways to customize your railing system to make it look fresh and different from other decks. One dramatic step you can take is to choose an unusual material option for the balusters. Balusters are available in various metals, including aluminum, stainless or powder-coated steel, copper, and iron. Metal balusters are fabricated in straight or contoured styles as well as turned and architectural profiles. They install into holes in wooden top and bottom rails or attach with screws. Strips of tempered glass are another baluster option, and they fasten in place with screws or slip into grooves in the rails. Or, fill the spaces between posts and rails with brightly colored outdoor fabric. It can be ordered with metal grommets installed so you tie it in place with weather-resistant rope.

If you use metal balusters, consider adding a centerpiece baluster between them. These unique balusters are made in various fleur de lis, classic, and nouveau patterns. They'll add shape and distinctiveness to your baluster pattern.

Wooden posts need not be drab, either. One option is to cover them with composite or vinyl sleeves in various colors or outfit them with a sleeve that looks like stacked stone. Instead of running hand rails over the top of your deck posts, let them extend above the railings and install post caps or decorative wood finials. Caps and finials simply fit over the tops of posts and nail or screw in place. Caps are widely available from home centers in copper or stainless steel. You can also order them made from stained glass or as low-voltage solar lights. Then, add a little flair to the bottoms of your posts with one-piece, composite trim skirts in decorative profiles.

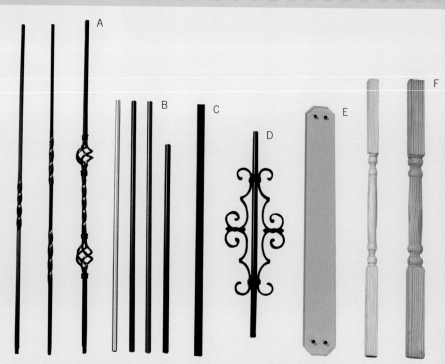

Balusters are available in a variety of styles and material options. Metal balusters are fabricated into many contoured profiles (A). You can also buy tubular styles (B) made of aluminum, stainless steel, and copper, or with a painted finish. Flat-bar balusters (C) or decorative centerpiece balusters (D) are other options, as well as strips of tempered glass (E). Wood balusters (F) are more economical than other styles, but they still lend a nicely crafted touch.

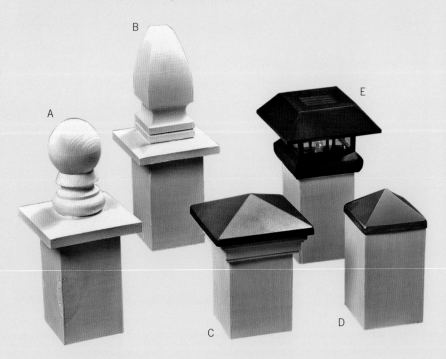

Dress up your deck railing posts with decorative top caps. You'll find them in various ball (A) and finial (B) shapes. Consider topping off your posts with paint (C) or copper (D), or maybe low-voltage or solar powered cap lights (E). Top caps will also help your wooden posts last longer by preventing water from wicking down into the end grain, leading to rot.

Post caps are available in a variety of styles made of metal, composites, or wood. Aside from adding a decorative touch, they also extend the life of the posts by keeping the end grain of the posts dry.

If you'd prefer not to build your railing from scratch, you can buy PVC or other composite railing systems that are long lasting and simple to install. Another advantage is you'll never need to stain or paint them.

Tempered-glass or Plexiglas panels are an excellent choice if your deck offers an impressive view. There are no balusters or handrails to peek through or over—just clear "windows" to the world beyond.

Contoured metal balusters will give your deck a fresh, contemporary twist. They attach with screws, just like wooden balusters.

Spindle-style, turned balusters are available in various metal tones and colors. They can lend a tailored effect to wooden railings, but they require the added work of fabricating top and bottom rails with mounting holes.

Ordinary wooden deck balusters can make you feel like you're "behind bars," but they're not the only option anymore. Today's tempered-glass balusters offer the same safety as wood but with the added advantage of a view.

Composite + PVC Railing Systems

M̲ost large composite or PVC decking manufacturers also offer complete railing systems to match the deck. You can use composite railings with a composite deck for a unified look, or use them with your wood deck as an easier, low-maintenance alternative to wood railings. Synthetic railings are sold both as complete sections and by the part, which allows you to customize the railings to suit your deck. Modern composite railings are offered in a wide range of styles, colors, and even textures, such as simulated wood grain. Balusters are just as diverse, ranging from simple posts, to tubes, to transparent acrylic panels. The diversity of looks, ease of installation, and the fact that material requires little if any care after installation all account for the quickly growing popularity of this railing material.

TOOLS + MATERIALS

Tape measure	Ratchet and sockets or impact driver	Lag screws	Stringers
Level	Miter saw	Posts	Ear and eye protection
½ × 6" hex bolts, washers, and nuts	16-gauge pneumatic nailer	Balusters	Work gloves
Drill/driver	Bracket tool	Rail cap	

Composite deck railing systems are very durable, easy to install and require only minimal maintenance.

How to Install a Composite Railing

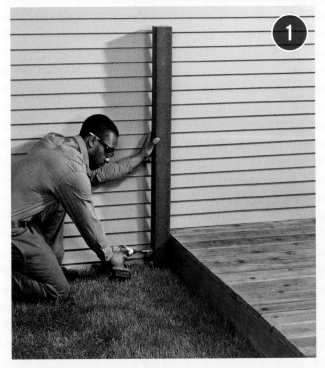

Fasten composite railing posts to the deck rim joists with pairs of ½"-diameter countersunk bolts, washers, and nuts. Position the posts 72" on center. Do not attempt to notch the posts.

Install railing support brackets, if applicable, to the posts using corrosion-resistant deck screws. For the railing system shown here, an assembly-bracket tool sets the placement of the brackets on the posts without measuring.

Assemble the railing sections on a flat surface. Again, the assembly tool shown here sets the spacing of the balusters. Fasten the bottom and top rails—in that order—to balusters with 16-gauge pneumatic nails or screws, according to the manufacturer's instructions.

Place the assembled railing section onto the railing support brackets and check it for level. Drive pairs of deck screws up though the support bracket holes and into the handrail. Toenail the bottom rail to the post with 16-gauge pneumatic nails.

Glass-panel Railings

For the ultimate in unobstructed viewing, you can install a glass-panel railing system on your deck and avoid balusters altogether. The system shown here is quite manageable to install without special tools. It consists of a framework of aluminum posts, and top and bottom rails that fasten together with screws. Extruded vinyl liner inserts that fit inside the top and bottom rails hold the glass without fasteners. Tempered-glass panels that are at least ¼-inch thick will meet building codes, provided the railing posts are spaced 5 feet on center. Some manufacturers offer poly-carbonate panels that are easier to work with and satisfy most building codes, although it can be scratched and may cloud over time. With a system such as the one shown here, you assemble the railing framework first, then measure and order the glass panels to fit the rail openings.

Tempered-glass panels are both do-it-yourself friendly and code approved, provided you install them according to manufacturers' guidelines.

How to Install a Glass-panel Railing

Once you've determined the layout of the deck posts, fasten the post brackets to the deck with lag screws. Install all the posts before proceeding.

Measure the length of the top rail inner channels, and cut glass insert strips to fit. Fasten the glass rail brackets to the posts with screws.

Insert the top post sleeves into the post ends, then measure and cut the top rails to length. Assemble the rails and sleeves, fastening the parts with screws. Check each post for plumb with a level before driving the attachment screws, and adjust if necessary.

Measure the distance between the glass insert strips and add ¾" to this length to determine the height of the glass panels. Measure the distance between posts and subtract 3 to 6" from this measurement to find the glass panel width, less air gaps. Order your glass. Install the bottom rails on the brackets.

Slip each glass panel into the top insert, swing it into place over the bottom insert and lower it into the bottom channel to rest on the rubber setting blocks. No further attachment is required.

Steel Cable Railings

Another railing option that can open up the view from a deck—not to mention give the deck some distinctive style—is to use braided steel cables run horizontally between posts. Lengths of cables are run continuously through holes in the posts and tension is created with special threaded fittings on the ends of the cable runs. Cables are spaced 3 inches apart or less, with railing posts spaced 3 feet on center. Most people purchase complete railing systems with prefabricated metal posts as shown here. Do not use wood posts with cable railings. In any case, the posts need to be securely fastened to the decking to resist the tension in the cables. A sturdy top rail is used with special fasteners to stabilize the railing and provide additional lateral reinforcement. Because of the tension inherent in cable railings, always follow the manufacturer's instructions to the letter.

YOUR CABLE SYSTEM

There are many ways to create a cabled railing. The complete system shown here is one of the easiest; the manufacturer supplies all the parts you need with complete, code-compliant instructions. Installation is easy, even for someone with modest skills. However, the cost of a system like this can become prohibitive if your deck is large. Other systems involve cables run between turnbuckles bolted or screwed to the posts. These require more work, and you have to be careful to install a sturdy top plate between posts to oppose the tension of the cables. The simplest system involves eyehooks screwed into the posts, and cables threaded through the eyehooks. Whichever you choose, it is extremely important when thinking about cabled railings to check with the local building inspector. Some localities prohibit horizontal cables—and horizontal balusters of any kind—because they can be climbed.

TOOLS + MATERIALS

Measuring tape	Wrenches
Level	Electric grinder
Drill/driver	Cable-lacing needle
Hacksaw	Ear and eye protection
Cable cutters	Work gloves
Self-locking pliers	

A series of braided steel cables can replace ordinary wood balusters and give your deck a clean, contemporary look. Posts must be spaced closely together to handle the cable tension and ensure safety.

How to Install Cable Railings

If you install flanged metal posts, secure them to the deck's framing with stainless steel lag screws and washers.

Drill holes through the railing posts to fit the cables, threaded end fittings, and quick connect locking fittings. Pass the terminal threaded ends of the cables through one railing end post and install washer nuts about ¼" onto the threads.

Feed the cables through the intermediate posts and the opposite end post. Work systematically to prevent tangling the cables. A cable-lacing needle will make it easier to pass cables through each post without snagging it. Attach cap rails (inset).

Slip a self-locking fitting over the end of each cable and seat the fitting in the cable hole in the post. You may need to counterbore this hole first to accommodate the fitting. Pull the cable tight. Jaws inside the fitting will prevent the cable from becoming slack again.

Tighten each cable nut with a wrench, starting from the center cable and working outward. A locking pliers will keep the cable from twisting as you tighten the nut. Tighten the nut until you cannot flex the cables more than 4" apart.

Cut off the excess cable at the quick-connect fitting end with a cable cutter or hacksaw. Grind the end of the cable flush with the fitting, and cover it with a snap-on end cap.

Advanced Framing Techniques

The majority of decks built today are fairly similar: a rectangular surface between 120 and 200 square feet, attached to your house with a ledger board and supported by posts and a beam. Access is usually a straight three- to five-step set of deck stairs, with a wood baluster railing. But of course this model is not for everyone or every situation. Sometimes, by necessity or by choice, things get more complicated.

The most crucial part of any deck-building project is the framing. Once you break out of the typical deck footprints, the system of support takes on a whole new set of challenges. Multilevel decks, decks with long staircases and multiple landing, curved and angled decks . . . all of these decks require design and construction skills that are more advanced, if not more difficult.

In this chapter, we'll show you examples of decks that are framed to accomplish specific tasks and solve specific challenges. It is unlikely that your advanced deck project will resemble any of these completely (or even closely), but follow along and you'll see some techniques and methods that we're sure you can use in your own deck design. As always, and particularly with an advanced project, work closely with your building inspector and don't be afraid to pull in help from a professional deck designer or even a structural engineer. The risks of getting in over your head when building an elevated structure like a deck are quite real.

In this chapter:
- Framing Low-profile Decks
- Framing Multilevel Decks
- Framing Decks on Steep Slopes
- Working with Angles
- Creating Curves
- Framing for Insets

Framing Low-profile Decks

Building a deck that sits very close to the ground is generally easier than constructing a very high deck, but low-profile situations do require some design modifications. If the deck is extremely low (8 to 12 inches high), it is best to rest the beams directly on the concrete footings, since posts are not practical. The joists usually are hung on the faces of the beams

rather than resting on top of the beams; cantilever designs are rarely used. Since the ledger is mounted so low on the house, it may need to be anchored to the foundation wall rather than to the home's rim joist.

A deck that is more than 12 inches above the ground should have at least one step–either box-frame style or suspended from the deck.

Beams for a low-profile deck often rest directly on concrete footings, with no posts. Because low-profile decks may require 2 × 8 or 2 × 6 joists, an intermediate beam may be required to provide adequate support for these narrower joists. At each end of the last beam, the outside timber must be 1½" longer than the inside timber, creating a recess where the end of the rim joist will fit.

How to Install Low-profile Beams + Joists

(1)

(2)

Install the ledger, then lay out and dig footings. If beams will rest directly on footings, use tube forms. Raise the tubes to the proper height and check them for plumb as you pour the concrete. Smooth off the surfaces of the footings, and insert direct-bearing hardware while the concrete is still wet, using layout strings to ensure that the hardware is aligned correctly.

Construct beams (page 97), then set the beams into the direct-bearing hardware. Drill pilot holes and use 4" through bolts (or manufacturer's recommendation) to secure the beam to the hardware. Mark joist locations on the faces of the beams, then install joist hangers.

(3)

Cut and install all joists, attaching them with joist-hangers. Complete your deck using standard deck-building techniques. Install a box-frame or suspended step, if desired (see page 129).

Framing Multilevel Decks

NOTE

Multilevel decks are complex structures that require very specific construction methods and engineering. There is no reason an ambitious DIYer cannot build a multilevel deck. It is essential, however, that you work with a professional engineer to design the deck framing. Even better, consider hiring a professional deck builder to frame the deck. You can still save plenty of money and participate in the construction by laying decking, building guard railings, and adding any of a host of custom deck details.

The multilevel deck featured here is shown for demonstration purposes to give you an idea of what is involved in projects of this type. The specific construction details may or may not be allowed in your area, as code regulations vary from region to region.

Multilevel Support Strategies

The shared-beam method has one beam supporting both platforms where they overlap. The upper platform rests directly on the beam, while the lower hangs from the face of the beam. This method is an economical choice, since only one beam is required, and it is well suited for relatively flat building sites where the deck levels are close together.

The support-wall method features a top platform supported by a stud wall that rests on the lower platform, directly over the beam and posts. Unlike the methods listed above, the support-wall method requires that the lower deck platform be built first. This method is a good choice when you want to use decorative wall materials, such as cedar siding, to cover the gap between the two platforms. The support-wall method also works well if you want to complete your deck in phases, delaying construction of the upper level.

How to Install Shared-Beam Support

Joist location

Final cut-off

1

Beam location

After laying out and installing the ledger and all posts and footings, mark the posts to indicate where the beam will rest. Use a straight 2 × 4 and a level to establish a point that is level with the top of the ledger, then measure down a distance equal to the height of the joists plus the height of the beam. Cut off the posts at this point using a reciprocating saw.

2

Position a post-beam cap on each post. Construct a beam from 2 × 10 or 2 × 12 dimension lumber (page 97), then position the beam in the post-beam caps. If the beam is crowned, install it so the crowned side is up. Secure the post-beam caps to the posts and beam with joist hanger nails or screws.

(3)

Lay out joist locations for the upper platform on the ledger and on the top of the beam, then use a carpenter's square to transfer joist marks for the lower platform onto the face of the beam. Attach joist hangers at the joist layout lines on the ledger.

(4)

Measure, cut, and install joists for the upper platform, leaving a 1½" setback to allow for the thickness of the rim joist. At the beam, secure the joists by toenailing with 16d galvanized nails.

(5)

Attach joist hangers for the lower platform along the face of the beam, using a scrap piece of lumber as a spacer. Cut and install the joists for the lower platform.

(6)

Cut rim joists for both the upper and lower platforms, and attach them to the ends of the joists by endnailing with 3 16d nails. Complete the deck using standard deck-building techniques.

How to Install a Deck Support Wall

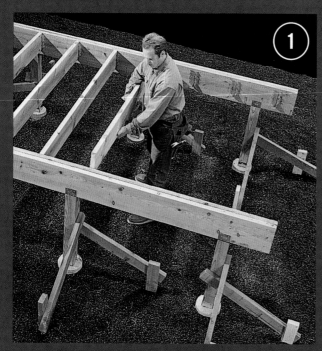

Lay out and install the ledger and all posts and footings, then frame the lower platform, using standard deck-building techniques.

Use a straight 2 × 4 and a level to establish a reference point level with the bottom of the top-level ledger, then find the total height for the support wall by measuring the vertical distance to the top of the lower platform. Cut the wall studs 3" less than this total height, to allow for the thickness of the top and bottom plates.

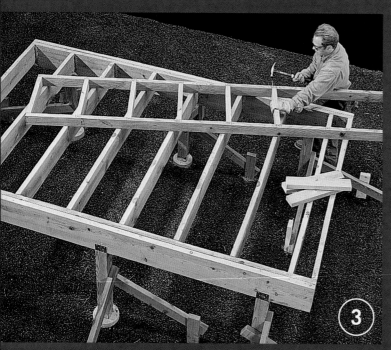

Cut 2 × 4 top and bottom plates to cover the full width of the upper platform, then lay out the stud locations on the plates, 16" on center. Cut studs to length, then assemble the support wall by endnailing the plates to the studs using galvanized 16d nails.

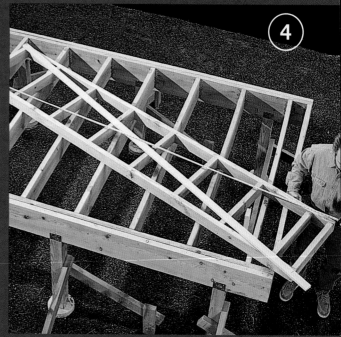

Set a long "sway" brace diagonally across the stud wall, and nail it near one corner only. Square the wall by measuring the diagonals and adjusting until both diagonal measurements are the same. When the wall is square, nail the brace at the other corner and to each stud. Cut off the ends of the brace flush with the plates.

Raise the support wall into position, aligning it with the edge of the beam and the end of the deck. Nail the sole plate to the beam with 16d galvanized nails driven on both sides of each stud.

Adjust the wall so it is plumb, then brace it in position by nailing a 1 × 4 across the end stud and outside joist.

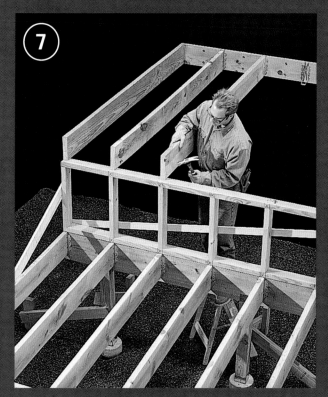

Lay out joist locations for the upper platform, and install joist hangers on the ledger. Cut joists so they are 1½" shorter than the distance from the ledger to the front edge of the wall. Install the joists by toenailing them to the top plate with 16d nails. Remove the braces.

Measure and cut a rim joist, and attach it to the ends of the joists by endnailing with 16d nails. Also toenail the rim joist to the top plate of the support wall. Complete the deck using standard deck-building techniques.

Framing Decks on Steep Slopes

Constructing a deck on a steep slope can be a complicated job if you use standard deck-building techniques. Establishing a layout for posts and footings is difficult on steeply pitched terrain, and construction can be demanding when one end of the deck is far above your head.

Professional deck contractors adapt to steep slope situations by using a temporary post-and-beam support structure and by slightly altering the construction sequence. Rather than beginning with post-footing layout, experienced builders begin by constructing the outer frame and raising it onto a temporary support structure. Once the elevated frame is in position, the locations of the permanent posts and footings can be determined.

In most instances, you will need helpers when building a deck on a steep slope. To raise and position the deck frame on temporary supports, for example, you will need the help of three or four other people.

NOTE: The steep-slope deck construction shown on the following pages was built using primarily 4 × 4 inch posts. Changes to building codes may require 6 × 6 inch posts. Always check with your local building department for applicable codes for your deck.

Another important consideration when building a deck on a steep slope is the composition of the soil. The slope needs to be stable and suitable for anchoring deep footings. If the earth is loose, rocky or prone to erosion, have it inspected by a geo-technical engineer first to make sure it will safely support a deck. The slope may need to be stabilized in other ways before construction begins.

If building the deck will require working at heights, use temporary support ledgers and bracing to prevent falls from ladders. Consider installing scaffolding, which may be a better solution than ladders if

The directions on the following pages show the construction of a deck featuring a corner-post design, but the technique can easily be adapted to cantilevered decks.

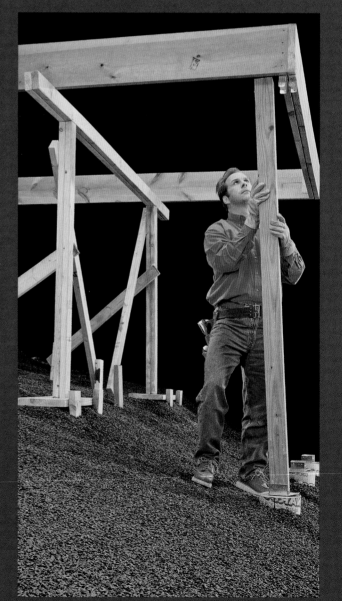

Building Decks on Slopes

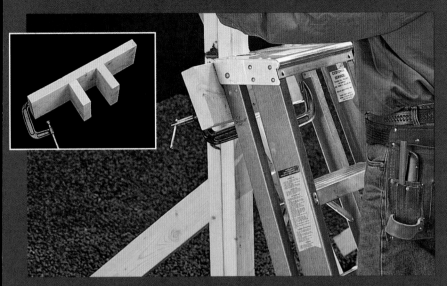

Stepladders should be used in the open position only if the ground is level. On uneven ground you can use a closed stepladder by building a support ledger from 2 × 6 scraps (inset) and clamping it to a post. Lean the closed ladder against the ledger, and level the base of the ladder, if necessary (below). Never climb onto the top step of the ladder.

Extension ladders should be leveled and braced. Install sturdy blocking under ladder legs if the ground is uneven or soft, and drive a stake behind each ladder foot to keep it from slipping. Never exceed the weight limit printed on the ladder.

Scaffolding can be rented from rental centers or paint supply stores. When working at heights, scaffolding offers a safer, more stable working surface. Place blocking under the legs of the scaffolding, and level it by screwing the threaded legs in or out.

How to Build a Deck on a Steep Slope

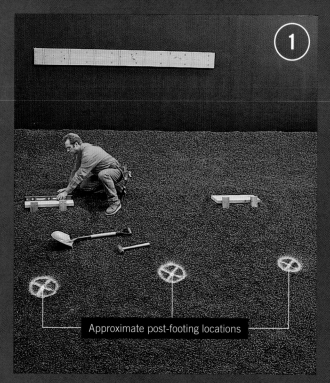

After installing the ledger, use spray paint or stakes to mark the approximate locations for the post footings according to your deck plans. Lay two 2 × 12 scraps on the ground to support temporary posts. Level the scraps and anchor them with stakes. The bases for the temporary posts should be at least 2' away from post-footing locations.

Approximate post-footing locations

Construct two temporary posts by facenailing pairs of long 2 × 4s together. Erect each post by positioning it on the base and attaching a diagonal 2 × 4 brace. Toenail the post to the base.

Attach a second diagonal brace to each post, running at right angles to the first brace. Adjust the posts until they are plumb, then secure them in place by driving stakes into the ground and screwing the diagonal braces to the stakes.

Mark a cutoff line on each post by holding a long, straight 2 × 4 against the bottom of the ledger and the face of the post, then marking the post along the bottom edge of the 2 × 4. Cut off the posts at this height using a reciprocating saw.

Construct a temporary support beam at least 2' longer than the width of your deck by facenailing a pair of 2 × 4s together. Center the beam on top of the posts and toenail it in place.

Build the outer frame of your deck according to your construction plans, and attach joist hangers to the inside of the frame, spaced 16" on center. With several helpers, lift the frame onto the temporary supports and carefully move it into position against the ledger.

NOTE: On very large or high decks, you may need to build the frame piece-by-piece on top of the temporary supports.

(continued)

Check to make sure the frame is square by measuring each side diagonally. If the measurements are not the same, adjust the frame on the temporary beam until it is square. Also check the frame to make sure it is level; if necessary, shim between the temporary beam and the side joists to level the frame. Toenail the frame to the temporary beam.

Use a plumb bob suspended from the deck frame to stake the exact locations for post footings on the ground.

NOTE: Make sure the footing stakes correspond to the exact center of the posts, as indicated by your deck plans.

Dig and pour footings for each post. While the concrete is still wet, insert J-bolts for post anchors, using a plumb bob to ensure that the bolts are at the exact center of the post locations. Let the concrete dry completely before continuing.

Check once more to make sure the deck frame is square and level, and adjust if necessary. Attach post anchors to the footings, then measure from the anchors to the bottom edge of the deck beam to determine the length for each post.

NOTE: If your deck uses a cantilever design, make sure to allow for the height of the beam when cutting the posts.

Cut posts and attach them to the beam and footing with post-beam caps and post anchors. Brace the posts by attaching 2 × 4 boards diagonally from the bottom of the post to the inside surface of the deck frame. Remove the temporary supports, then complete the project using standard deck-building techniques.

Working with Angles

Decks with geometric shapes and angled sides have much more visual interest than basic square or rectangular decks. Most homes and yards are configured with predictable 90° angles and straight sides, so an angled deck offers a pleasing visual surprise.

Contrary to popular belief, elaborate angled decks are relatively easy to plan and build, if you follow the lead of professional designers. As professionals know, most polygon-shaped decks are nothing more than basic square or rectangular shapes with one or more corners removed. An octagonal island deck, for example, is simply a square with all four corners omitted.

Seen in this light, complicated multilevel decks with many sides become easier to visualize and design.

For visual balance and ease of construction, use 45° angles when designing an angled, geometric deck. In this way, the joinery requires only common cutting angles (90°, 45°, or 22½°), and you can use skewed 45° joist hangers, readily available at home centers.

NOTE: The angled deck construction shown on the following pages was built using primarily 4 × 4 inch posts. Changes to many building codes require 6 × 6 inch posts. Always check with your local building department for applicable codes for your deck.

Joists on a cantilevered deck can be easily marked for angled cuts by snapping a chalk line between two points on adjacent sides of the deck corner. Marking and cutting joists in this fashion is easier than measuring and cutting the joists individually. To help hold the joists in place while marking, tack a brace across the ends. Mark joist locations on the brace for reference. The amount by which joists may cantilever (overhang) a beam is calculated using engineering tables and site-specific data about your plan. Engage a structural engineer to make these calculations for you.

How to Build an Angled Deck Using the Corner-post Design

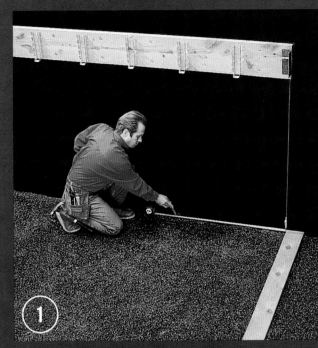

Use boards to create a rectangular template of the deck. To ensure that the template is square, use the 3-4-5 triangle method: From the corner directly below the ledger, measure 3' along the foundation, and mark a point. Measure out along the template board 4', and mark a second point. Measure diagonally between the two points. This measurement should be 5'; if not, adjust the template to square it.

Indicate each angled edge by positioning a board diagonally across the corner of the template. To ensure that the angles measure 45°, make sure the perpendicular legs of the triangle have exactly the same measurement. Nail the boards together where they overlap.

Mark locations for post footings with stakes or spray paint. At each 45° corner, mark locations for two posts positioned about 1' on each side of the corner. Temporarily move the board template then dig and pour the concrete footings.

While the concrete is still wet, reposition the template and check to make sure it is square to the ledger. Use a nail to scratch a reference line across the concrete next to the template boards, then insert J-bolts in the wet concrete. Let the concrete dry completely. *(continued)*

Attach metal post anchors to the J-bolts, centering them on the reference lines scratched in the concrete. The front and back edges of the anchors should be parallel to the reference line.

Measure and cut beam timbers to size. On ends that will form angled corners, use a speed square to mark 22½° angles on the tops of the timbers, then use a combination square to extend cutting lines down the face of the boards. Use a circular saw set for a 22½° bevel to cut off the timbers, then join them together with 16d nails.

Set posts into the post anchors, then use a mason's string and line level to mark cutoff lines on the posts at a point level with the bottom of the ledger. Cut off the posts, using a circular saw. Attach post-beam caps to the posts, then set the beams into place. Secure beam corners together with adjustable angle brackets attached to the inside of each corner with joist-hanger nails.

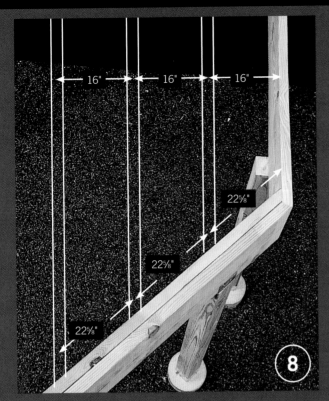

Measure and mark joist locations on the ledger and beams. If your joists are spaced 16" on center along the ledger, they will be spaced 22⅝" apart measured along the angled beam. If they are spaced 24" on center at the ledger, the joists will be spaced 33⁵⁄₁₆" apart along the angled beam.

Attach joist hangers at the layout marks on the ledger and beam. Use skewed 45° joist hangers on the angled beam.

Cut and install joists, securing them with joist-hanger nails. Joists installed in skewed 45° joist hangers can be square cut; they need not be beveled to match the angle of the beam. Complete the deck using standard deck-building techniques.

Creating Curves

By their nature, curved shapes lend a feeling of tranquility to a landscape. A deck with curved sides tends to encourage quiet relaxation. A curved deck can also provide an effective visual transition between the sharp architectural angles of the house and the more sweeping natural lines of the surrounding landscape.

Curved decks nearly always use a cantilevered design, in which the curved portion of the deck overhangs a beam that is set back from the edge of the deck. The amount by which joists may cantilever (overhang) a beam is calculated using engineering tables and site-specific data about your plan. Engage a structural engineer to make these calculations for you.

If your curved deck will be high enough to require a railing, we recommend a design that incorporates a circular curve rather than an elliptical or irregular curve. Adding a curved railing (pages 154 to 157) is much easier if the deck curve is based on a circular shape.

NOTE: The curved deck shown on the following pages was built using primarily 4 × 4 inch posts. Changes to building codes may require 6 × 6 inch posts. Always check with your local building department for applicable codes for your deck.

A curved deck is created by cutting joists to match the curved profile, then attaching a curved rim joist, which can be shaped in one of two ways (opposite page). Braces attached to the tops of the joists hold them in place as the rim joist is installed.

CURVES AND DECK DESIGN

Adding curves to your deck is not something you should do on the spur of the moment. Consider the pros and cons carefully before you commit to curves. Here are some to think about:

Pros:

- Curves can add visual appeal and uniqueness to your deck.

- Curves soften the overall feeling.

- Used wisely, curves have a natural, organic visual quality.

- A curve can be used to work around an obstacle in a pleasing way.

- A curved corner can preserve space below the deck.

Cons:

- Decks that incorporate curves almost always require more posts and beams, and they make less efficient use of building materials.

- A deck with curves takes at least twice as long to build as a square or rectangular one.

- Curved railings are tricky to make.

- Impact is lessened if curves are overused.

- Curves reduce and constrict deck floor space.

Design Options for Curved Decks

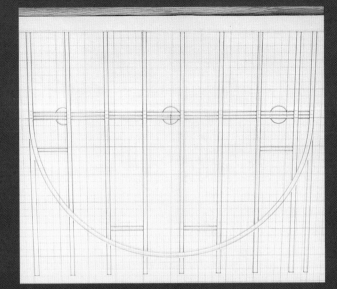

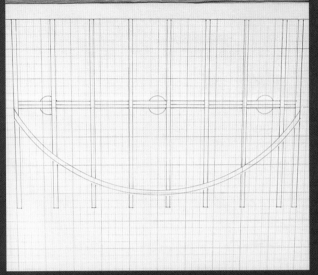

Circular designs are the best choice for curved decks that require railings. However, circular curves require a fairly long cantilever, which may limit the overall size of your deck and may butt up against the requirements of the local building code. Be sure to check your plans with local officials. Circular decks are laid out using simple geometry and a long compass tool, called a trammel, which you can make yourself.

Irregular or elliptical curves should be used only on relatively low decks, since railings are quite difficult to construct for this kind of curve. These designs also work well for large decks, since the amount of overhang on the cantilever is relatively short compared to that for a circular curve.

Construction Options

A kerfed rim joist is formed by making a series of thin vertical cuts (kerfs) across the inside face of the board, making it flexible enough to wrap around the curve. A kerfed rim joist made from 2"-thick dimension lumber is sufficiently strong, but if you are kerfing a 1"-thick redwood or cedar fascia board, it should be backed with a laminated rim joist (photo, right).

Laminated rim joist is made by bending several layers of flexible ¼"- or ⅜"-thick exterior-grade plywood around the curve, joining each layer to the preceding layer with glue and screws. A laminated rim joist can stand alone, or it can provide backing for a more decorative fascia, such as a kerfed redwood or cedar board.

How to Lay Out a Curved Deck

Install posts and beam for a cantilevered deck. Cut joists slightly longer than their final length, and attach them to the ledger and the beam. Add cross-blocking between the two outside joists to ensure that they remain plumb.

Mark the joist spacing on a 1 × 4 brace, and tack it across the tops of the joists at the point where the deck curve will begin. Measure the distance between the inside edges of the outer joists at each end of the beam, then divide this measurement in half to determine the radius of the circular curve. Mark the 1 × 4 brace to indicate the midpoint of the curve.

Build a trammel by anchoring one end of a long, straight 1 × 2 to the centerpoint of the curve, using a nail. (If the centerpoint lies between joists, attach a 1 × 4 brace across the joists to provide an anchor.) Measure out along the arm of the trammel a distance equal to the curve radius, and drill a hole. Insert a pencil in the hole and pivot the trammel around the centerpoint, marking the joists for angled cuts.

VARIATION: For elliptical or irregular curves, temporarily nail vertical anchor boards to the outside joists at the start of the curve. Position a long strip of flexible material, such as hardboard or paneling, inside the anchor boards, then push the strip to create the desired bow. Drive nails into the joists to hold the bow in position, then scribe cutting lines on the tops of the joists.

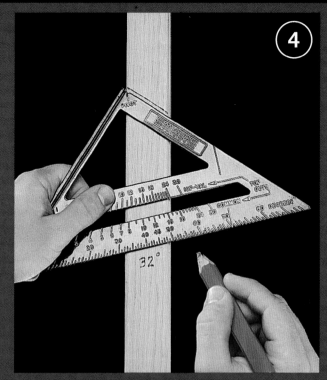

Use a speed square or protractor to determine the bevel angles you will use to cut the joists. Position the square so the top is aligned with the layout mark on the joist, then find the degree measurement by following the edge of the joist down from the pivot point and reading where it intersects the degree scale on the square.

Use a combination square to extend the cutting lines down the front and back faces of the joists. At the outside joists where the curve begins, mark square cutting lines at the point where the circular curve touches the inside edge of the joists.

Cut off each joist with a circular saw set to the proper bevel. Clamp a straightedge to the joist to provide a guide for the foot of the saw. On the outside joists where the curve begins, make 90° cuts.

Where the bevel angle is beyond the range of your circular saw, use a reciprocating saw to cut off the joists.

How to Construct a Kerfed Rim Joist for a Curved Deck

Blocking

Mark the inside face of the rim joist lumber with a series of parallel lines, 1" apart. Using a circular saw or radial-arm saw set to a blade depth equal to ¾ of the rim joist thickness (1⅛" for 1½"-thick lumber), make crosscut kerfs at each line. Soak the rim joist in hot water for about 2 hours to make it easier to bend.

Install a cross block between the first two joists on each side of the curve, positioned so half the block is covered by the square-cut outside joist (inset). While it is still damp, attach the rim joist by butting it against the end joist and attaching it to the cross block with 3" deck screws. Bend the rim joist so it is flush against the ends of the joists, and attach with two or three 3" deck screws driven at each joist.

Additional cross block

Where butt joints are necessary, mark and cut the rim joist so the joint falls at the center of a joist. To avoid chipping, cut off the rim joist at one of the saw kerfs.

Complete the installation by butting the end of the rim joist against the outside joist and attaching it to the cross block. Use bar clamps to hold the rim joist in position as you screw it to the blocking.

NOTE: If the rim joist flattens near the sides of the deck, install

How to Construct a Curved Rim Joist with Laminated Plywood

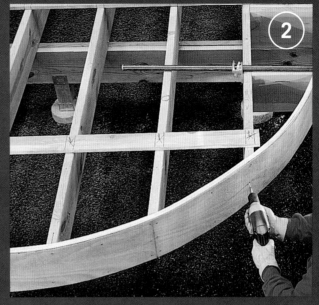

Install blocking between the first two joists on each side of the deck (step 2, previous page). Cut four strips of ¼"-thick exterior plywood the same width as the joists. Butt the first strip against the outside joist and attach it to the blocking with 1⅝" deck screws. Bend the strip around the joists and attach with deck screws. If necessary, install additional blocking to keep the plywood in the proper curve. If butt joints are necessary, make sure they fall at the centers of joists.

Attach the remaining strips of plywood one at a time, attaching them to previous layers with 1" deck screws and exterior wood glue. Make sure butt joints are staggered so they do not overlap previous joints. For the last layer, use a finish strip of ⅜" cedar plywood. Where the finish strip butts against the outside joists, bevel-cut the ends at 10° to ensure a tight fit.

 How to Install Decking on a Curved Deck

Install decking for the square portion of the deck, then test-fit decking boards on the curved portion. If necessary, you can make minor adjustments in the spacing to avoid cutting very narrow decking boards at the end of the curve. When satisfied with the layout, scribe cutting lines on the underside of the decking boards, following the edge of the rim joist.

Remove the scribed decking boards and cut along the cutting lines with a jigsaw. Install the decking boards with deck screws, and smooth the cut edges of the decking boards with a belt sander or random-orbit sander, if necessary.

Framing for Insets

If your planned deck site has a tree, boulder, or other large obstacle, you may be better off building around it rather than removing it. Although framing around a landscape feature makes construction more difficult, the benefits usually make the effort worthwhile. A deck with an attractive tree set into it, for example, is much more appealing than a stark, exposed deck built on a site that has been leveled by a bulldozer.

The same methods used to frame around a preexisting obstacle also can be used to create a decorative or functional inset feature, such as a planter box, child's sandbox, or brick barbecue. On a larger scale, the same framing techniques can be used to enclose a hot tub or above-ground pool.

A framed opening can also provide access to a utility fixture, such as a water faucet, electrical outlet, or central air-conditioning compressor. Covering a framed opening with a removable hatch preserves the smooth, finished look of your deck.

Inset framing makes it possible to save mature trees when building a deck. Keeping trees and other landscape features intact helps preserve the value and appearance of your property. Check with a tree nursery for an adequate opening size for any tree you want to contain within an inset.

Large insets that interrupt joists can compromise the strength of your deck. For this reason, inset openings require modified framing to ensure adequate strength. Double joists on either side of the opening bear the weight of double headers, which in turn support the interrupted joists. Always consult your building inspector for specifics when constructing a deck with a large inset.

How to Frame for an Inset

Rough-frame the opening by using bolted double joist hangers to install double joists on each side of the inset, and double headers between these joists. Install the interrupted joists between the double headers and the rim joist and ledger.

Modify your deck plan, if necessary, to provide the proper support for the interrupted joists in the inset opening. If the inset will interrupt one or two joists, frame both sides of the opening with double joists. If the opening is larger, you may need to install additional beams and posts around the opening to provide adequate support. Consult your building inspector for specific requirements for your situation.

Inset box shown cutaway for clarity.

Where needed, cut and install angled nailing blocks between the joists and headers to provide additional support for the decking boards. When trimmed, decking boards may overhang support members by as much as 4" around an inset opening.

VARIATION: An inset box can be used as a planter for flowers or herbs. Build the box from ¾"-thick exterior-grade plywood, and attach it to the framing members with deck screws. A deep box can be supported by landscape timbers. Line the inside of the box with layers of building paper, then drill ½"-wide holes in the bottom of the box to provide drainage. To keep soil from washing out through drainage holes, line the box with landscape fabric.

Custom Deck Projects

Creating your own custom deck or customizing an existing deck is a fun and rewarding process. The scale of the projects you pursue can range from building a simple freestanding deck on concrete supports to designing and building an entire brand-new deck attached to your house.

The preceding pages of this book showed you practically everything you need to know to design and build a deck yourself. The pages in this chapter present specific projects that are great examples of ways you can put the information you've learned to work.

The first two projects show you in full step-by-step detail how to enclose the area beneath a second-level deck to make a weatherproof and bugproof outdoor living area. Next is a very simple but attractive low-profile deck that is built directly onto an unappealing concrete patio. Finally, a freestanding, octagonal deck platform is constructed. Because it is not attached to a permanent structure and it is low to the ground, it requires only precast concrete piers for support.

Not all custom deck projects require sawing and fastening. The final project in this chapter offers suggestions for expanding the functionality of your deck simply by adding furnishings or appliances.

In this chapter:
- Underdeck Enclosure
- Runoff Gutters
- Boardwalk Deck on a Slab
- Floating Octagon Island Deck
- A Deck for Entertaining

Underdeck Enclosure

TOOLS + MATERIALS

4' level	Underdeck ceiling system
Chalk line	Waterproof acrylic caulk
Caulking gun	1" stainless steel screws
Drill	Rain gutter system
Hacksaw (for optional	(optional)
rain gutter)	Ear and eye protection
Aviation snips	Work gloves

Second-story walkout decks can be a mixed blessing. On top, you have an open, sun-filled perch with a commanding view of the landscape. The space below the deck, however, is all too often a dark and chilly nook that is functionally unprotected from water runoff. As a result, an underdeck area often ends up as wasted space or becomes a holding area for seasonal storage items or the less desirable outdoor furniture.

But there's an easy way to reclaim all that convenient outdoor space—by installing a weatherizing ceiling system that captures runoff water from the deck above, leaving the area below dry enough to convert into a versatile outdoor room. You can even enclose the space to create a screened-in patio room.

The underdeck system featured in this project is designed for do-it-yourself installation. Its components are made to fit almost any standard deck and come in three sizes to accommodate different deck-joist spacing (for 12, 16, and 24 inches on-center spacing). Once the system is in place, the underdeck area is effectively "dried in," and you can begin adding amenities like overhead lighting, ceiling fans, and speakers to complete the outdoor room environment.

The system works by capturing water that falls through the decking above and channeling it to the outside edge of the deck. Depending on your plans, you can let the water fall from the ceiling panels along the deck's edge, or you can install a standard rain gutter and downspout to direct the water to a single exit point on the ground or a rain barrel. Steps for adding a gutter system are given on pages 197 to 205.

Made of weather-resistant vinyl, this underdeck system creates an attractive, maintenance-free ceiling that keeps the space below dry throughout the seasons.

Design Tips

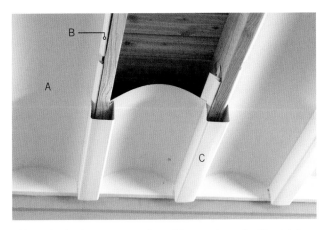

This underdeck system consists of four main parts: The joist rails mount to the deck joists and help secure the other components. The collector panels (A) span the joist cavity to capture water falling through the deck above. Water flows to the sides of the panels where it falls through gaps in the joist rails (B) and into the joist gutters (C) (for interior joists) and boundary gutters (for outer joists). The gutters carry the water to the outside edge of the deck.

For a finished look, paint the decking lumber that will be exposed after the system is installed. Typically, the lower portion of the ledger board (attached to the house) and the outer rim joist (at the outer edge of the deck) remain exposed.

Consider surrounding architectural elements when you select a system for sealing off the area below your deck. Here the underdeck system is integrated with the deck and deck stairs both visually and functionally.

How to Install an Underdeck System

Check the undersides of several deck joists to make sure the structure is level. This is important for establishing the proper slope for effective water flow.

If your deck is not level, you must compensate for this when setting the ceiling slope. To determine the amount of correction that's needed, hold one end of the level against a joist and tilt the level until it reads perfectly level. Measure the distance from the joist to the free end of the level. Then, divide this measurement by the length of the level. For example, if the distance is ¼" and the level is 4' long, the deck is out of level by 1/16" per foot.

To establish the slope for the ceiling system, mark the ends of the joists closest to the house: Measure up from the bottom 1" for every 10' of joist length (or approximately ⅛" per foot) and make a mark. Mark both sides of each intermediate joist and the inside faces of the outer joists.

Create each slope reference line using a chalk line: Hold one end of the chalk line at the mark made in step 3, and hold the other end at the bottom edge of the joist where it meets the rim joist at the outside edge of the deck. Snap a reference line on all of the joists.

Install vinyl flashing along the ledger board in the joist cavities. Attach the flashing with 1" stainless steel screws. Caulk along the top edges of the flashing where it meets the ledger and both joists, using quality waterproof acrylic caulk. Also caulk the underside of the flashing for an extra layer of protection.

Begin installing the joist rails, starting 1" away from the ledger. Position each rail with its bottom edge on the chalk line and fasten it to the joist at both ends with 1" stainless steel screws, then add one or two screws in between. Avoid overdriving the screws and deforming the rail; leaving a little room for movement is best.

Install the remaining rails on each joist face, leaving a 1½" (minimum) to 2" (maximum) gap between rails. Install rails along both sides of each interior joist and along the insides of each outside joist. Trim the final rail in each row as needed, using aviation snips.

Measure the full length of each joist cavity, and cut a collector panel ¼" shorter than the cavity. This allows room for expansion of the panels. For narrower joist cavities, trim the panel to width following the manufacturer's sizing recommendations. *(continued)*

Trim panel here

Scribe and trim collector panels for a tight fit against the ledger board. Hold a carpenter's pencil flat against the ledger, and move the pencil along the board to transfer its contours to the panel. Trim the panel along the scribed line.

Trim the corners of collector panels as needed to accommodate joist hangers and other hardware. This may be necessary only at the house side of the joist cavity; at the outer end, the ¼" expansion gap should clear any hardware.

Install the collector panels, starting at the house. With the textured side of the panel facing down, insert one side edge into the joist rails, and then push up gently on the opposite side until it fits into the opposing rails. When fully installed, the panels should be tight against the ledger and have a ¼" gap at the rim joist.

Prepare each joist gutter by cutting it ¼" shorter than the joist it will attach to. If the joists rest on a structural beam, see Working Around Beams, on page 202. On the house end of each gutter, trim the corners of the flanges at 45°. This helps the gutter fit tightly to the ledger.

13

Cut four or five ⅛" tabs into the bottom surface at the outside ends of the gutters. This helps promote the drainage of water over the edge of the gutter.

14

Caulk here

Attach self-adhesive foam weatherstrip (available from the manufacturer) at the home-end of each joist gutter. Run a bead of caulk along the foam strip to water-seal it to the gutter. The weatherstrip serves as a water dam.

15

Install each joist gutter by spreading its sides open slightly while pushing the gutter up onto the joist rails until it snaps into place. The gutter should fit snugly against the collector panels. The gutter's home-end should be tight against the ledger, with the ¼" expansion gap at the rim joist.

16

Prepare the boundary gutters following the same steps used for the joist gutters. Install each boundary gutter by slipping its long, outside flange behind the joist rails and pushing up until the gutter snaps into place. Install the boundary gutters working from the house side to the outer edge of the deck. *(continued)*

Run a bead of color-matched caulk along the joint where the collector panels meet the ledger board. This is for decorative purposes only and is not required to prevent water intrusion.

If collector panels are misshapen because the joist spacing is too tight, free the panel within the problem area, then trim about ⅛" from the side edge of the panel. Reset the panel in the rails. If necessary, trim the panel edge again in slight increments until the panel fits properly.

WORKING AROUND BEAMS

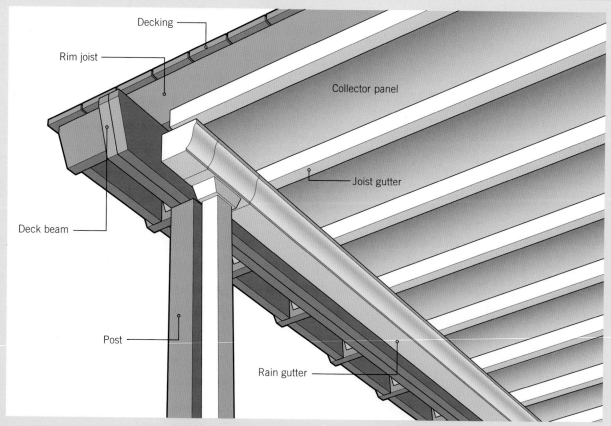

Decking

Rim joist

Collector panel

Joist gutter

Deck beam

Post

Rain gutter

For decks that have joists resting on top of a structural beam, stop the joist gutters and boundary gutters 1½" short of the beam. Install a standard rain gutter along the house-side of the beam to catch the water as it exits the system gutters. (On the opposite side of the beam, begin new runs of joist gutters that are tight against the beam and stop ¼" short of the rim joist. The joist rails and collector panels should clear the beam and can be installed as usual.) Or you can simply leave the overhang area alone if you do not need water runoff protection below it.

Runoff Gutters

A basic gutter system for a square or rectangular deck includes a straight run of gutter channel with a downspout at one end. Prefabricated vinyl or aluminum gutter parts are ideal for this application. Gutter channels are commonly available in 10- and 20-foot lengths, so you might be able to use a single channel without seams. Otherwise, you can join sections of channel with special connectors. Shop around for the best type of hanger for your situation. If there's limited backing to support the back side of the channel or to fasten into, you may have to use strap-type hangers that can be secured to framing above the gutter.

How to Install an Underdeck Runoff Gutter

Snap a chalk line onto the beam or other supporting surface to establish the slope of the main gutter run. The line will correspond to the top edge of the gutter channel. The ideal slope is 1/16" per foot. For example, with a 16'-long gutter, the beginning is 1" higher than the end. The downspout should be located just inside the low end of the gutter channel. Mark the beam at both ends to create the desired slope, then snap a chalk line between the marks. The high end of the gutter should be just below the boundary gutter in the ceiling system.

(continued)

Install a downspout outlet near the end of the gutter run so the top of the gutter is flush with the slope line. If you plan to enclose the area under the deck, choose an inconspicuous location for the downspout, away from traffic areas.

Install hanger clips (depending on the type of hangers or support clips you use, it is often best to install them before installing the gutter channel). Attach a hanger every 24" so the top of the gutter will hang flush with slope line.

 GUTTER OPTIONS ● ● ● ● ● ● ● ● ● ●

Gutters come in several material types, including PVC, enameled steel, and copper. In most cases you should match the surrounding trim materials, but using a more decorative material for contrast can be effective.

Cut sections of gutter channel to size using a hacksaw. Attach an end cap to the beginning of the main run, then fit the channel into the downspout outlet (allowing for expansion, if necessary) and secure the gutter in place.

Join sections of channel together, if necessary, using connectors. Install a short section of channel with an end cap on the opposite side of the downspout outlet. Paint the area where the downspout will be installed if it is unpainted.

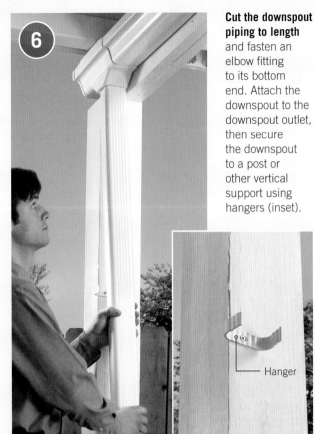

Cut the downspout piping to length and fasten an elbow fitting to its bottom end. Attach the downspout to the downspout outlet, then secure the downspout to a post or other vertical support using hangers (inset).

Hanger

Cut a drain pipe to run from the downspout elbow to a convenient drainage point. Position the pipe so it directs water away from the house and any traffic areas. Attach the pipe to the downspout elbow. Add a splash block, if desired.

REROUTING DOWNSPOUTS

You may have to get a little creative when routing the downspout drain in an enclosed porch or patio. Shown here, two elbows allow for a 90° turn of the drainpipe.

Boardwalk Deck on a Slab

There's no need to let a cracked, aging concrete patio ruin the look and enjoyment of your backyard. You can build a very simple deck platform right over the failing slab with very little effort or expense. Make no mistake, though: the result will be a beautiful new outdoor platform that improves the look of the home and the yard.

This is an independent deck—the structure is not attached to the house, but is instead laid atop the slab and allowed to move with any shifting in the concrete. It's constructed on a simple frame base laid level with sleepers over the concrete itself. This means that the deck will be very close to the ground and subject to a great deal of moisture. Only certain types of decking will tolerate those conditions. We've used pressure-treated pine decking.

The design of the deck is a plain rectangle and can easily be constructed over a weekend. We've spruced up the look a bit by laying the decking in a standard "boardwalk" pattern. More complex patterns would make the deck surface look even more impressive— just remember to do yourself a favor and work the patterns out on graph paper before cutting any decking. Proper planning will inevitably save a lot of waste.

Turn a boring or failing concrete slab into an attractive walkout or entertainment space with a short utility or "boardwalk" deck installed on top of it.

CUTAWAY VIEW

SUPPLIES

Galvanized metal corner brackets (16)

2½" galvanized deck screws

2" composite shims

Circular saw

Miter saw

Power drill and bits

Treated lumber (2 × 4 and 2 × 2)

8" plastic shims

Construction adhesive

Caulk gun

Level

Deck stain

Paintbrush

Ear and eye protection

Work gloves

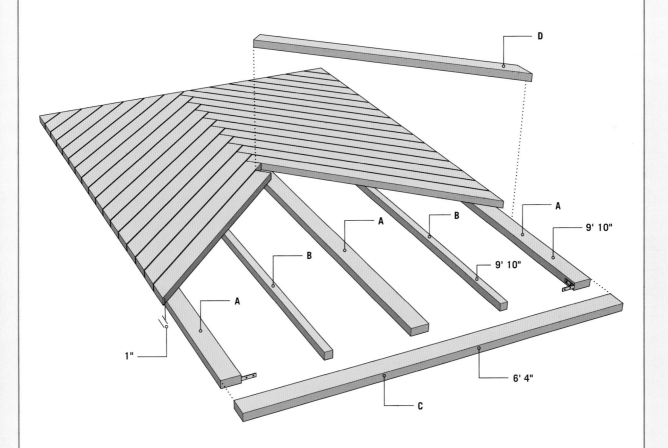

CUTTING LIST

KEY	QTY	SIZE	PART	MATERIAL
A	3	1½ × 3½ × 128"	Frame side	PT pine
B	2	1½ × 1½ × 128"	Nailer	PT pine
C	2	1½ × 3½ × 76"	Frame end	PT pine
D	60	1½ × 3½ × (cut to fit)	Decking	PT pine

How to Build a Boardwalk Deck

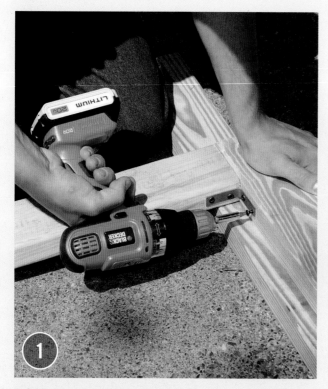

Build and assemble the frame offsite by cutting and measuring 10' 2 × 4s to length and securing them together with galvanized metal corner brackets.

Install the nailer joists by measuring and cutting parallel boards to the length of the frame. Use 2" deck screws and galvanized metal corner brackets to secure the nailer joists to the frame.

Clear away any dust and debris from the concrete slab. Set the frame atop the slab and use 8" plastic shims to level it. Glue shims in place.

Use a level as you work with the shims to ensure an even plane on which to build the deck.

Remove the frame from the slab before installing the decking. Stagger the 2 × 4s in a crosshatch pattern in opposing 45° angles from the center nailing joist. Attach the boardwalk pattern to the frame using 3" deck screws. Boards should abut one another the length of the joist and allow for at least 1" of overhang from the frame.

Mark 1" overhang on all sides of the frame using a chalk-line, and cut off excess decking using a circular saw equipped with a carbide blade.

Use a helper to install the decking atop the concrete slab, checking for level and using shims to adjust as necessary.

Clear away dust and debris and stain the decking as desired.

Floating Octagon Island Deck

Sometimes all you need is a simple, easy-to-build platform to complete an otherwise perfect backyard. The project shown here is an "island deck," detached from the house and requiring no ledger attachment.

That means it has the simplest of foundations; a set of precast concrete pier blocks that are simply set in place, making them far easier to work with than poured footings. The piers are cast to a standardized shape and size: 10 inches square and 10 inches high, with slots in the top to accommodate joists and posts. Because the pier blocks are not secured in the ground, the deck "floats." This allows for movement in response to settling and the freeze-thaw cycle of the soil. Floating pier decks meet most local codes—but check yours just to be sure.

This deck is also low enough to the ground that it won't require a handrail (unless, in your particular case, the yard severely slopes off to one side).

DESIGN TIPS

This deck would be ideal when accessorized with a three-sided privacy screen (pages 234 to 237) to serve as a wind barrier for easy grilling. You could also add double benches (pages 238 to 243) along the side opposite the privacy screen, so you'll have ample seating for guests to relax while their steaks are cooking. The only way for this deck to be more convenient is if the steaks grilled themselves!

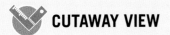

SUPPLIES

Preformed concrete pier blocks (25)

Tape measure

Level

3" galvanized deck screws

Circular saw

Miter saw

Power drill and bits

Stain or sealer

Ear and eye protection

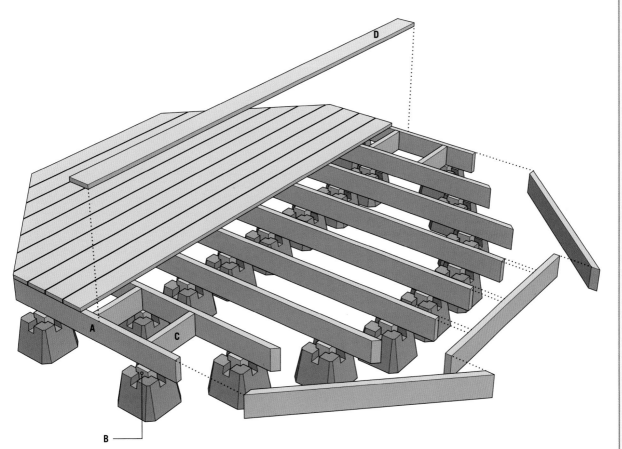

Overall size: 10 × 10 ft.

CUTTING LIST

KEY	QTY	SIZE	PART	MATERIAL
A	8	1½ × 5½ × 49¾"	Joist	PT pine
B	25	3½ × 3½ × (cut to fit)	Post	PT pine
C	6	1½ × 5½ × 13½"	Spreader	PT pine
D	22	1½ × 5½ × (cut to fit)	Decking	PT pine

FRAMING PLAN

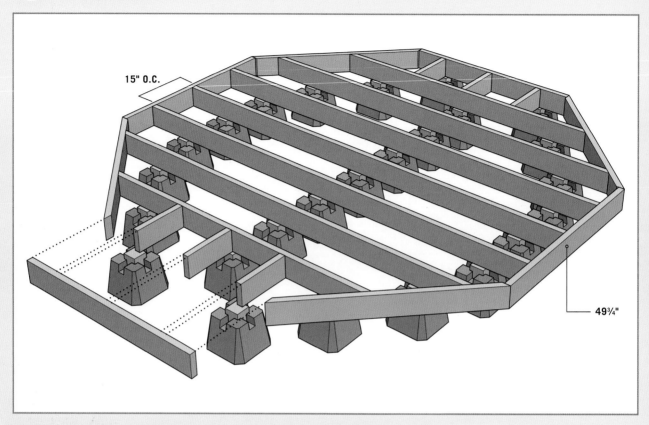

15" O.C.

49¾"

DECKING DETAIL

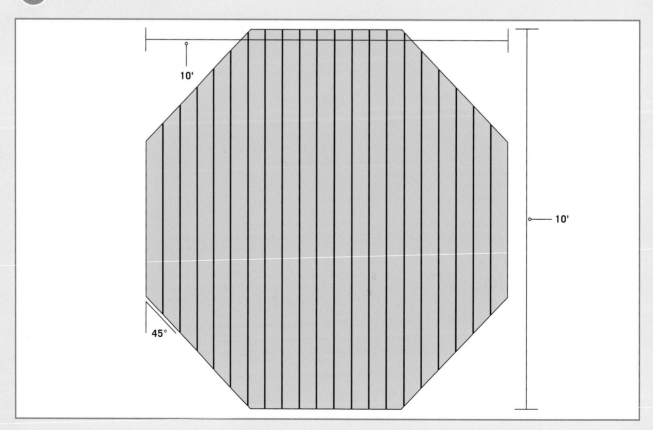

10'

10'

45°

How to Build a Floating Octagon Island Deck

Clear the deck area of rocks and debris. Measure, mark, and place the pier blocks, starting with three rows of three to form the center "box." Ensure the blocks are level both ways. (The rows here were placed 46½" OC row to row.) Add or remove dirt under the blocks to ensure level block to block.

Set a 10' 2 × 6 on edge in the pier block slots on one side of the row. Check level with a helper, raising or lowering the joist as needed. Measure any gaps with the joists held level.

Cut slices of 4 × 4 to match the measurements and place them under the joists where there are gaps, checking level once again. Repeat the process with the joist on the opposite side. Finally, make sure the joists are level side to side.

(continued)

Cut two 2 × 6 band joists 49¾" long. Measure and mark the band joists at each end of the joists to ensure that the overhang on both sides is equal. Screw the band joists to the floor joists with 3" deck screws. This creates the center box.

Check that the center box is square by measuring the diagonals. Measure twice and check carefully because the accuracy of this box determines the measurements of the rest of the deck.

Position and level the center joist in the box, using cut pieces of 4 × 4 as necessary to raise the joist at a pier block. Check level side to side with the outside floor joists. Once the center joist is level both ways, screw it to the band joist with 3" deck screws.

Measure, place, and level the remaining pier blocks according to the plan on page 212. Cut and position the shorter outside floor joists in the octagon (which sit in the same position, but perpendicular to, the band joists). Level them in place as before.

Screw the outside joists in position to the blocking, if any. Double-check the measurements of the pier blocks as you've arranged them, and the on-center measurements of the joists. *(continued)*

Measure and cut the shorter remaining joists that will be placed between the box and the outside joists. Miter the ends 22½° before installing. Level them in position as before. Measure and cut the remaining band joists, mitering each end 22½°. Screw the band joists to the joists. Join the band joists at the miters by drilling pilot holes and then screwing them to complete the outer frame. Add blocking (spreaders) as per the framing plan on page 212. (Not shown in photos.)

Begin laying the decking along one edge of the octagon with the decking perpendicular to the joists. Position the first deck board with its outside edge aligned with the edge of the band joist. Screw the board down using two 3" deck screws at each deck. Leave the overhang on each end to be trimmed at the end of construction.

Continue laying the decking, leaving a consistent ⅜" expansion gap between boards (use spacers to make the work go quicker). Place each board with roughly equal overhang on each side of the deck and screw in place.

Use a circular saw equipped with a carbide blade to trim off the deck-board overhangs flush with the edge of the band joists. Add on any built-in structures such as benches or planters, and then seal, stain, paint, or finish the deck and other wood surfaces, including the band joists, as you prefer.

A Deck for Entertaining

Outdoor entertaining on a deck often involves preparing a meal. If the menu is just burgers and hot dogs, most of that food prep takes place at the grill. But even the simplest fare still involves those inevitable trips back and forth to the kitchen to toss a salad, warm up a side dish, or replenish the cold drinks. More complex meals will keep the chef in the kitchen even longer—and that means less time spent out on the deck with family and friends. Wouldn't it be great if you could bring the kitchen to the deck to take care of more—or even all—of those food prep tasks?

At one time, outdoor kitchens were still more fantasy than reality, but that's no longer the case. Today, Americans are increasingly seeing their decks as important outdoor entertainment areas, and not just places to park the patio table and grill. An assortment of custom grills, outdoor appliances, and storage cabinets can help you transform your deck into a fully functional kitchen. These appliances are UL-listed and designed for outdoor use, so your kitchen doesn't have to be located in a covered porch or tucked under a roof. You can cook and prepare right where you serve. Outdoor appliances are generally more expensive than their indoor cousins, but if outdoor entertaining is an important part of your lifestyle, you can now enjoy it more fully than ever before and without compromise.

Imagine the dinner parties you could host if your deck had a fully functional outdoor kitchen! It's a trend in outdoor entertaining that continues to grow in popularity. These days, there are outdoor appliances to suit most kitchen tasks.

Whether you use your deck for intimate outdoor dining, boisterous parties, or quiet conversation, decks provide an ideal way to extend your home's dining space into the outdoors.

A sturdy outdoor patio table and chairs, made of suitable exterior-rated wood or metal, is a beneficial improvement to any deck. Tables that accept large shade umbrellas are even more practical, especially if your deck is located in a sunny spot.

A high-end outdoor kitchen with stainless steel appliances and solid wood cabinetry leaves no question that this deck owner is serious about food.

Outdoor Appliances

For years, better-quality grills have included a sideburner and second grate to keep food warm. Now, you can purchase expansive grilling stations that may include dedicated infrared warming drawers, storage cabinets and drawers, insulated cubbies for ice, and extended serving counters. They're a relatively affordable way to take your grilling and food preparation tasks to the next level, and you can buy these units at most home centers.

Self-contained grilling stations are just one of many appliance options to choose from. For more culinary convenience, you can also buy outdoor-rated ovens, multi-burner rangetops and refrigerators, ice makers, and beverage coolers from a number of reputable manufacturers. Ovens and rangetops are heated by either propane or natural gas, depending on the model. They're designed as modular components that fit into a bank of cabinets or a custom-built kitchen island. Outdoor refrigerators are relatively compact and nest under a countertop where they can be at least partially sheltered from the elements. They range in capacity from around 3 to 6 cubic feet. Outdoor sinks, wet bars, and dedicated food-prep stations are other options you might consider adding to your deck kitchen.

A variety of outdoor kitchen appliances, such as refrigerators, ice makers, and wine coolers, can help keep food and drinks cold no matter how hot the day may be.

Custom barbecue islands
can be configured in lots of different ways to suit your space and food prep needs. The primary appliance is generally a gas grill with a cabinet underneath for storing the LP tank. A bank of drawers provides handy places to keep grilling tools and other cooking utensils or spices.

A warming drawer outfitted in your barbecue island can help you stage various dinner items while you grill the main course. Some prefabricated barbecue islands include a warming drawer.

This self-contained beer keg cooler will keep your favorite brew cold on the hottest summer day and for as long as the party lasts. All it takes is an electrical outlet.

Consider adding a plumbed sink to your outdoor kitchen. It will make food prep and clean-up much easier. Be sure to check with local building codes concerning running hot and cold supply lines or installing an appropriate drain.

If your barbecue grill isn't equipped with a side burner, it's an essential feature you'll want to add to your outdoor kitchen. Side burners are available as independent accessories that can be built into a kitchen island or bank of cabinets.

Cabinets + Countertops

Once you step beyond a one-piece grilling station, you'll need to store a stove, refrigerator, or other appliances in a system of cabinets or an island base of some kind. This could be as simple as an enclosed framework with a countertop, or it can be as elaborate as you like. Chances are, you'll want to include a few storage cabinets and drawers to keep utensils, cookware, and other supplies close at hand. Some cabinet manufacturers offer weather-resistant cabinets made from teak, cypress, mahogany, or other exterior woods. They're available as modular components that can be mixed and matched like other cabinetry. Polyethylene, marine-grade polymer, or stainless steel cabinets are more options to consider: they're corrosion-resistant, waterproof, and hypoallergenic. It's a good idea to buy your appliances first, then design an island or bank of cabinets that will fit what you own.

A variety of countertop materials could make a durable and attractive serving surface for your kitchen. Porcelain tile is weather-resistant and affordable, and it's manufactured in virtually any style and color you can dream of. You could choose a fabricated countertop made of stainless steel, soapstone, granite, or marble. Or, build your counter from a piece of tempered glass. If your deck kitchen will be sheltered under an awning or roof, solid-surface material is also good choice. However, the polymer blends that make up solid-surface materials aren't formulated to be UV stable, and they could deteriorate over time.

If you build your own countertop, be sure to start with a substrate layer of cement backer board if you use grouted tile or other permeable material. It will prevent water from seeping through to appliances or into storage cabinets.

If you're a competent woodworker, consider building custom cabinets to outfit your deck kitchen rather than buying them. Make them from the same wood as your other patio furniture or decking so they blend into your deck scheme perfectly.

Building an Island Base

For handy do-it-yourselfers, designing a weatherproof kitchen island can offer a hearty challenge and an excellent chance to explore some new building materials. Start with a framework of pressure-treated or cedar lumber, and sheathe it with waterproof cement backer board. Then, cover the exposed surfaces with patio tile, stucco, veneered stone or brick. Or, use exterior plywood as the substrate for your island framework, then follow with vinyl, fiber cement, or cedar lap siding to match the siding of your house. You could even use composite decking to sheathe your kitchen island or grilling station so it visually ties in with your deck's design. Or, wrap the outside in sheets of stainless steel or aluminum for a sleek, modern look.

You'll want to expand the storage capabilities of your deck kitchen by including a variety of cabinets. Exterior-grade cabinets are made with durable polymers, rot-resistant woods, or stainless steel, and they are available in a range of sizes and styles to suit your needs.

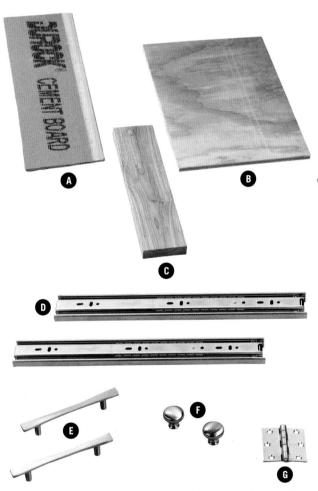

Choose water-resistant building materials for the structural and sheathing components of your island. Cement board (A), outdoor woods like cedar or redwood (B), and exterior-rated plywood (C) are all suitable home-center options. For cabinets, choose corrosion-resistant drawer slides (D), drawer hardware (E, F), and hinges (G).

BUILD OR HIRE?

Depending on where you live, you might be able to hire a contractor to design and build the countertop, base, and cabinets for your deck appliances. However, given that deck kitchens are still a relatively new concept, you may need to carry out these projects on your own. Companies that sell outdoor appliances and cabinetry may be able to help you design your outdoor deck kitchen. You can also find grilling station and island project designs in outdoor kitchen design books.

Keep in mind that you may need to run a natural gas line and several ground-fault protected outlets to the kitchen. If you decide to include a functional sink in your design, you'll need at least one potable water line and possibly a sanitary drain that empties into a dry well or your home's plumbing system. Be sure to install these utilities so that they conform to the building codes in your area. The proper course of action is to apply for the appropriate utility permits and have the work inspected. If you are in doubt of your skills with running gas lines or wiring electrical receptacles, have this work performed by a licensed plumber and electrician.

Soapstone is a moderately hard, natural material that works well for exterior countertop applications. The stone is semi-porous, so it should be periodically sealed if it's exposed to the elements. Sealing helps maintain water resistance.

Granite is an excellent countertop material. It's much harder than soapstone and available in many natural colors and surface textures. Common varieties of granite are in the same price range as soapstone.

Concrete is more affordable than natural stone, and it can be tinted in a wide range of colors or mixed with other aggregates to add texture and visual interest. Another benefit to concrete is that it can be poured to suit any shape of countertop you may need.

Grouted patio tile will also work well for an outdoor kitchen countertop. It's inexpensive, easy to install without special skills, and comes in many sizes, colors, and styles. You'll need to seal the grout periodically if the countertop is exposed to the elements or has a sink.

IS YOUR DECK WELL SUITED FOR A KITCHEN?

A deck kitchen may sound like an intriguing notion, but think carefully about the ramifications of dedicating part of your deck to this purpose. You'll need a certain amount of counter space for preparing food and staging it for cooking or storing it while you cook. Do you want to reserve a portion of the counter area for dining, or will that take place at a separate patio table? Are your home's utilities close enough to the deck to make gas lines or plumbing convenient to run? Will a kitchen island, patio table, and other deck furniture all fit comfortably on your deck without making the space feel crowded? As you begin to plan your outdoor kitchen, it may help to use masking tape, pieces of plywood, or cardboard boxes to lay out a space for your kitchen. This will help you visualize how the size of the kitchen would impact the rest of your deck. Ultimately, an outdoor kitchen should enhance your outdoor entertaining options and make your deck more useful, not overwhelm it.

Deck Accessories

Accessorizing your deck is one of the most enjoyable parts of the deck-building process. It's your chance to add a feature such as a pergola or bench that can inject flair and help you personalize the structure. The variety of accessories available means adding to your deck will usually be limited only by your imagination and your budget.

Almost any accessory can be customized to suit your deck or house style. For example, low-voltage lighting makes the area safer and adds visual appeal. Go with a sleek and stunning modern bench design, or opt for a chunky, grounded look that adds a strong visual presence. Create a pergola of natural wood to blend with wood shingle siding, or use white composite to create one that offers a clean, fresh complement to light-colored vinyl siding.

Keep in mind that aside from the style, the accessory you choose will usually add function as well. Benches don't just embellish the deck's appearance or create a visual border along the edge; they also introduce incredibly useful seating. A planter not only stands out on its own, but it can also hold a small, lush herb garden that blurs the distinction between the deck and the landscaping and provides seasonings for the kitchen.

In this chapter:
- Low-Voltage Lighting
- Deck Planters
- Privacy Screen
- Deck Benches
- Deck Skirting

Low-voltage Lighting

Adding lights to your deck will not only extend the use of the deck after dark, but it will also make the area safer and, when done right, adds an eye-catching design element. Low-voltage lighting systems are easier to work with and safer than standard line voltage—the voltage that powers your inside lights and appliances. There is no need to bury the cable or encase it in conduit. Most systems simply plug into an outdoor outlet where a step-down transformer reduces the voltage from 120 down to about 12.

You can purchase individual components or complete kits that include the transformer, light fixtures, connectors, and cable.

How to Install Low-voltage Deck Lighting

1

To hide the cable in a deck railing post, route a shallow groove in the middle of the post. An alternative is to hide the cable in a groove in the top rail. Vinyl and metal railing systems often contain hollow sections that allow you to conceal the cable. Run cable from the location of the transformer, which is near an outdoor outlet, to the location of the lighting fixtures.

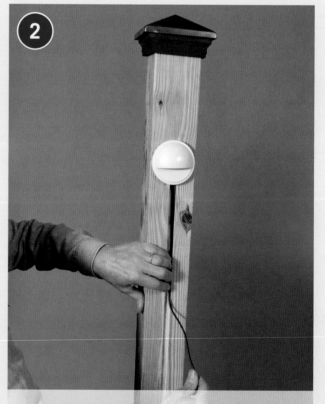

2

Attach the light fixture to the post and lay the cable in the groove. For added support, staple the cable to the post. You can connect individual post lights to the main cable underneath the deck. Most connections are made with snap-on connectors, so there is no need to splice wires.

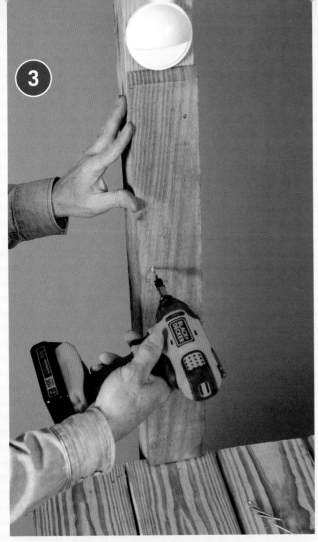

Drill a hole through the stair riser to install step lighting. For standard width steps, about 3 ft, one light per riser is usually sufficient. For wider stairs, use two or three fixtures. It looks best if the lights align when you are facing the steps.

Install a 1 × 4 cut to length to hide the cable, using corrosion-resistant screws. Install lights on the other posts.

Fish the wires for each fixture through the holes you drilled in the riser. You will be able to connect individual fixtures to the main system beneath the deck.

Attach the light fixture to the riser with the screws that come with the light kit or use corrosion-resistant screws. Place the lens cover in position and connect the fixture to the main cable.

Mount the step-down transformer near a GFCI electrical outlet as per the manufacturer's directions. Connect the main cable to the transformer. You will operate the system from the transformer, so it should be in a position that is easy to reach. You can also install a timer or a photocell so that the lights turn on at dusk and off and dawn.

Deck Planters

There is no better way to integrate your deck with the surrounding landscape than to build a planter right onto the deck's surface. You can use a built-in planter to create a mini-garden, or just to add splashes of color and key points on the structure. The planter itself is also a chance for you to inject some customized style to the structure.

The easiest planters to build are simple squares or rectangles like the one featured here. However, you shouldn't feel confined to those basic shapes; most planter plans can easily be adapted to just about any shape. That adaptability can come in handy when you need to tuck the planter into the odd corner of an unusual deck design.

Regardless of what shape you choose, it's always helpful to have some idea of what you want to plant in the planter. Different plants can require radically different types of soil and space for roots. A tree will require a much different planter than a small display of blooming annuals. In any case, it's wise to attach the planter to the deck to prevent it from falling over due to high winds or rambunctious party guests.

A planter like this is relatively easy to construct and adds immeasurably to the look of the deck, not only with its design, but also by hosting attractive plant life.

TOOLS + MATERIALS

Circular saw

Miter saw

Power drill + bits

Measuring tape

4 × 4 lumber

1 × 3 lumber

1 × 1 nailing strips

1 × 4 lumber

3" galvanized deck screws

2½" galvanized deck screws

¾" exterior-grade plywood

Nail set

Pond liner or 6-mil poly

Ear and eye protection

Work gloves

How to Build a Deck Planter

1

Use a miter saw or circular saw to cut all the framing members. Mark and cut four 4 × 4 legs and twenty 1 × 4 side panels, all 18" long. Cut four 1 × 2 rails 21" long, and four 14" long. Cut eight 1 × 1 nailing strips 14" long.

2

Assemble the end panels by laying four 1 × 4s side by side, aligning them perfectly. Lay a short 1 × 2 rail across one end, running it perpendicular to the boards. Drill pilot holes and screw the rail to each of the panel boards.

3

Position the nailing strips along the outside edges of the panel and drill pilot holes. Screw the nailing strips in place, and then screw the bottom rail in place as you did with the top rail. Butt it up against the bottom of the nailing strips (there should be a gap between the bottom edge of the rail and the bottom edges of the panel boards). Repeat the process using six 1 × 4s to construct the side panels.

4

Set a leg on the worktable and align a panel with the leg. Drill pilot holes through the nailing strip on the back of the panel, into the leg, and screw the panel to the leg using a screw every 2". Continue attaching the legs in the same manner until the box of the planter is complete.

(continued)

Cut a rectangle of exterior-grade ¾" plywood, 26½" × 19½". Notch the corners by cutting in 2¾" from each edge.

5

6

Turn the planter box upside down and screw the plywood bottom into place, drilling pilot holes at the edges into the bottom rails, and then screwing the bottom to the rails. Use a ¼" bit to drill holes in the center of the plywood to allow for drainage.

7

Cut the 1 × 4s for the plinth and top frame. Cut four 28" long, and four 21" long. Miter the ends of all pieces 45°.

8

Attach the planter box to the deck by measuring and setting it into position. Drive 2½" decking screws down through the plywood bottom and into the deck. Use one screw at each corner, located as close to the outer panel as possible.

Screw the plinth pieces in place around the base of the planter by driving 2" deck screws from the inside of the box, through the bottom rail and into the plinth piece. Use three screws per side.

Staple the planter box liner all around, attaching it over the top rail, but not so that it overlaps onto the outside of the side panels. Cut some holes in the bottom for drainage.

Drill pilot holes through the outside edges of the top frame pieces through the miters. Position the frame in place on the planter and drill pilot holes down through the frame and into the legs. Nail the frame in place with galvanized finish nails, and use a nailset to sink the nails.

Sand and finish the box if desired. Add a few inches of gravel at the bottom, then soil and plants. Water thoroughly.

Privacy Screen

TOOLS + MATERIALS

Measuring tape	finish nails
Power drill + bits	4 × 4 lumber
Miter saw	1 × 2 lumber
Jigsaw or circular saw	2 × 4 lumber
1⅜" spade bit	Exterior-grade ¾" lattice
5 × ½" lag screws	Pyramid or other post finial
+ washers	Construction adhesive
3" deck screws	Caulk gun
2½" deck screws	Ear and eye protection
1½" 4d galvanized	Work gloves

Today's deck has the potential to be much, much more than just a simple step-out platform. You can design your deck to be an outdoor dining room with a secluded nook for quiet, intimate meals, a discrete sunbathing platform, or a sanctuary to read the paper in peace and get away from it all. But for all of these, privacy is key. A romantic brunch is no fun when it's in direct view of a neighbor's yard or kitchen window. And that's where a privacy screen can come in mighty handy.

Deck-mounted privacy screens have to conform to the same codes—or in some cases, more stringent versions—that the deck railings do. You have to be very careful that the placement of a screen does not impede on an egress opening, and that the clearance around windows and vents is adequately maintained. If you live in an area subject to strong winds, code issues will be even more of a concern and the screen may require special reinforcement so that it can withstand added wind load. Ultimately, you may also have to install blocking between the joists running to where the screen is mounted, to help combat the stress from the wind load.

As important as code issues are, don't lose sight of the fact that a privacy screen is a substantial deck feature. Take the time to make sure the design adds to the look, as well as the function, of your deck.

A lattice privacy screen allows for airflow and some light to filter through and offers privacy from other yards. Privacy screens are not a substitute for guard railings.

How to Build a Privacy Screen

Measure and cut the 4 × 4 posts for the screen. Each post should be 6' 5" long. Miter the bottom ends of the posts to a 22½° angle. Seal the cut ends with a sealer-preservative, even if you're using pressure treated wood.

Measure and mark 2" up from the bottom of the backside of the posts, and 2" above that mark. Drill ⅜" pilot holes at those marks and then countersink each ½" with a 1⅜" spade bit.

Mark the locations of the top and bottom plates on the inside faces of the posts. Mark the post positions on the side of the deck and double check your measurements (the posts should be exactly 46" apart on center). Hold the posts in position and mark through the pilot holes for the joist holes.

Attach the privacy screen posts to the edge of the deck with the aid of a helper. Hold each post in place, checking plumb with a level, and use 5 × ½" lag screws and washers to connect the post to the deck.

(continued)

Cut the screen frame pieces from 1 × 2 stock: 2 side pieces 5' long and top and bottom pieces 43" long. Miter the ends of the framing pieces to 45°. Mark a 4 × 8 sheet of lattice and use a jigsaw or circular saw to cut the sheet down to 4 × 5.

Position the bottom plate between the two posts, using spacers to hold the plate in place. Screw the plate to the posts from the top, in toenail fashion, using two 3" deck screws on both sides.

Drill countersunk pilot holes in the edges of all the screen framing pieces for the 3" deck screws that will secure the frame to the posts and plates. Space the holes about 10" apart.

Assemble the front frame by clamping pieces at the mitered joints, drilling pilot holes for 2" deck screws. Measure diagonally after the frame is finished to ensure square. Assemble the rest of the frame in the same way, and repeat to construct the back frame.

9

Add the outside frame. Drill pilot holes into the post and attach with 3" deck screws.

10

Place the lattice in position and install the inner frame. Predrill and nail the inner to the outer frame through a lattice strip every 8" with 4d galvanized nails.

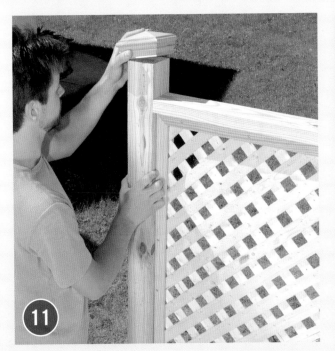

11

Screw the top plate into place, and screw the top frame pieces to the top plate and to each other. Finish the screen by covering the post tops with finials. The finials used here are glued to the post top with construction adhesive.

12

Add additional segments by repeating these steps and adding a 2 × 6 cap mitered at 22½° at the mated ends. This plate will replace the finials.

Deck Benches

TOOLS + MATERIALS

Tape measure	3 prefab braces and hardware
Circular saw	⅜" drill bit
Miter saw	Pressure treated 2 × 4s
Power drill	3" galvanized deck screws
4 × 4 lumber	2½" decking screws
1 × 4 lumber	5 × ⅜" lag screws
2 × 4 lumber	Bar clamps
2 × 6 lumber	Ear and eye protection
1" spade bit	Work gloves

A well-designed deck bench can often serve double duty. Installed along the perimeter of a low-lying deck, a long bench adds visual interest to what is often a fairly uninteresting uniform shape. Benches with built-in backs can stand in for railings on higher decks, ensuring the safety, as well as comfort, of everyone.

You can build fully enclosed deck benches to create useful additional storage—a handy way to hide sporting goods and cookout gear when they are not in use. Benches are also the perfect partner to planters, visually linking one or more independent mini-gardens.

Of course, the most important role any deck bench fulfills is that of accessible, durable, and comfortable seating on the deck. If you can measure accurately and operate a miter saw precisely, you can complete this bench in a weekend. It's a good idea to drive screws up through the underside of the deck into the legs so that the screws are completely invisible.

Improve the look and comfort of a deck with a built-in bench. Building one is fairly easy, whether you're retrofitting an existing deck or adding one as part of a brand-new platform.

How to Build a Deck-mounted Bench

Cut six 15"-long legs from 4 × 4s. Cut 3 bases from the same material as the legs. Each base should be 4" long.

1

2

Place a leg on the worktable with a scrap piece underneath. Mark and drill a 1" hole, ½" deep, 1½" up from the bottom of the leg on the outside face (use a depth gauge on a spade bit). Change to a ⅜" bit to complete the pilot hole, drilling a hole in the center of the larger hole, and through the other side of the leg.

3

Drill identical base holes on all the other legs. Place a base in position against the inside edges of two legs, aligned with the bottom of the legs. Stick a long thin spike, awl, or other marking device through the hole to mark the location of the pilot holes on each end of the base.

4

Remove the base and drill ¼" pilot holes into the ends at the marks. Repeat with all the bases and mark each base for the legs it goes with.

(continued)

Measure and cut the leg top plates. These can be pressure-treated 2 × 4s because they won't be visible once the bench is assembled. Cut three plates 16½" long. Make marks on the long edges of the plates 2¾" from each end.

Complete the leg assemblies by aligning the edge marks on each top plate with the outside edges of the legs, and drilling two pilot holes through the top of the plate into each leg. Attach the plates to the legs with 3" screws.

Cut three 2 × 6s, each exactly 6' long, for the seat. Lay them side by side, clamped together with the ends aligned. Mark the leg positions across the boards. The end leg units should be 2" from each end. The center leg unit should be centered along the span.

NOTE: Make attaching the legs to the decking easier and more secure by determining leg position along the deck before attaching them to the seat. Center each leg board on top of a decking board so that you can screw into the center of the board to secure the legs.

Set the leg assemblies in place, upside down on the 2 × 6s, using the marks for reference. Screw through the bottom of the top plates into the seat boards. Use two 2½" decking screws per 2 × 6, for each leg unit.

Cut two 2 × 4 side frame pieces 6' 3" long, and two end pieces 19½" long. Miter each edge 45° and dry fit the frame around the outside of the bench seat.

Assemble the frame by attaching the end pieces to the ends of the 2 × 6s and the side pieces to the pressure-treated top plates. Use 3" deck screws to secure the frame pieces in place. Drill pilot holes through the miters and screw the frame pieces to each other.

Position the bench on the deck. Mark the leg base locations. Remove the bench and drill pilot holes for each base, down through the base and deck board. Use a spade bit to countersink the holes. Drive ⅜" lag screws down through the bases into the deck boards. Put the bench into position and secure it to the bases using ⅜" lag bolts and washers.

For a more finished look, cut plugs from the same wood as the legs and glue them into place to cover the lag bolt heads in the sides of the legs. Sand as necessary and finish the bench with whatever finish you prefer.

VARIATION: How to Build an Edge-mounted Bench

This project is an edge-mounted bench built by using prefab braces (see Resources, page 268) that make constructing the bench much easier. It has a canted back that allows a person to lean back and relax, and is mounted right to the band joist, also called the rim joist. We've built this as a double bench, with mitered boards on one side so that the benches look like a continuous unit.

 ## TOOLS + MATERIALS

Power drill + bits	Prefab	2 × 4 lumber
Miter saw	deck braces	Ear and eye
Tape measure	+ hardware	protection
2½" deck screws	2 × 6 Lumber	Work gloves

Attach the first bracket centered along the band joist 6" from where the bench will end. Screw it to the decking and band joist using the 1½" screws and washers provided, screwing through the holes in the bracket.

Attach the second bracket on the band joist, no more than 24" away from the first bracket. Screw two brackets to the adjacent band joist in exactly the same pattern.

Measure and mark six 2 × 6s for the seats and top caps of the benches. The boards should be same width on the inside edge as the band joist, mitered out to the wider back edge 22½°, so that the members of each bench butt flush against each other.

Cut four 2 × 4 back supports 41" long. Miter the top ends 12°. Position each back support in a bracket, mark the 2 × 4 through the holes in the brackets, and drill for the mounting bolts. Attach the back supports with the 2½" bolts supplied, using washers on both sides.

Position the top cap on top of the back supports, leaving a ¾" overhang in the back. Drill pilot holes and screw the top caps to the back supports with 2½" deck screws, with the mitered edges meeting on the inside corner between the two bench segments. Screw the seat boards into position the same way, driving the supplied 1" screws up through the bottom of the leg brackets, into the 2 × 6 seat boards.

Measure and miter twelve 2 × 4 back and leg boards in the same way as you did the seat and top cap boards, but with the boards on edge. Butt the top back board up underneath the top cap, so that the mitered end is positioned on the inside corner between the two bench segments. Screw it into the back supports using 2½" deck screws. Attach the two remaining back boards in the same way, leaving a 2" gap between the boards.

Position the seat skirt on the front of the bench seat in the same way you positioned the seat boards. Mark and drill pilot holes, and screw the skirt to the front 2 × 6 using 2½" deck screws. Screw the leg boards into position, using 1" screws driven through the holes in the brackets and scrap 2 × 4 blocks on the flat as spacers.

Attach the back, seat, and leg boards on the adjacent bench section in the same way, making sure that the mitered edges leave a 1" gap between the two bench sections.

INSET: Install added support behind the back boards where the adjacent benches meet using scrap blocking and deck screws.

Deck Skirting

Elevated decks are often the best solution for a sloped yard or a multistory house. A deck on high can also take advantage of spectacular views. But the aesthetic drawback to many elevated decks is the view from other parts of the yard. The supporting structure can seem naked and unattractive.

The solution is to install deck skirting. Skirting is essentially a framed screen attached to support posts. Skirting creates a visual base on an elevated deck and adds a more finished look. It looks attractive on just about any deck.

There are many types of skirting. The project here uses lattice, perhaps the most common and easiest to install. But you can opt for solid walls of boards run vertically or horizontally. However, keep in mind that lattice allows for air circulation underneath the deck. If you install solid skirting, you may need to add vents to prevent rot or other moisture-related conditions under the deck. Codes also require that you allow access to egress windows, electrical panels, and other utilities under the deck, which may involve adding a gate or other structure to the skirting.

How To Install Deck Skirting

Determine the length of the skirting sections by measuring the space between posts. Measure on center and mark the posts. At corners, measure from the outer edge of the corner post to the center of the next post in line. Determine the height of the skirting by measuring from the top of a post to grade leaving at least 1" between the skirt bottom and ground.

Cut the top and side frame sections for the skirting from 1 × 4 pressure treated lumber. You can also use cedar or other rot- and insect-resistant material. Snap a chalk line 1" above the bottom of the post, and use a speed square to find the angle of the slope.

Cut the ends of the frame pieces to fit. Assemble the 1 × 4 frame using galvanized angle brackets.

Cut the ¾" lattice to dimensions of the frame, using a circular saw or jigsaw. Align the lattice on the back of the 1 × 4 frame, and screw the lattice to the frame about every 10" using 1" galvanized screws.

Install each finished lattice skirting section as soon as it is assembled. Align the edges of the frame with the marks you've made on the posts and drill pilot holes through the front of the frame and lattice into the post. Screw the section to the post with 3" galvanized deck screws, using a screw at the top, bottom, and middle of the frame.

OPTIONAL: If the length between posts is greater than 8', add stiles in the frame to support extra lattice panels. Cut 1 × 4 stiles to length so that they fit between the top and bottom rails. Screw it in place by using a 4" or larger T brace on the back of the frame. Then nail the lattice in place.

Once the skirting is installed, you can finish it to match the house or deck, or leave it natural if you prefer. Painting lattice will be much easier and quicker with a sprayer; rent one, or buy one if you have other large paint jobs on the schedule.

Finishing + Maintaining Your Deck

As outdoor structures, decks are constantly subjected to the elements, the wear and tear of foot traffic and use, and in some cases, damage from insects. To ensure that your deck lasts as long as possible, take steps to protect the surface and maintain the structural integrity. Wood decks should be treated with a protective finish every few years, which will keep the wood attractive and slow the damaging effects of the elements. Composite, metal, and plastic decking should be regularly and thoroughly cleaned.

Eventually, you may need to make more drastic structural repairs as your deck ages or structural issues arise. If you are diligent on the necessary upkeep and maintenance, your deck will last for decades.

This chapter will introduce you to the common cleaning and finishing products that are available for preserving wood decks. You'll learn how to apply finish to new wood and clean weathered or previously finished wood in preparation for refinishing. We'll show you how to inspect your deck for rotten wood, and walk you through the step-by-step process for replacing decking, joists, and rotten posts. We'll also outline how to clean composite and other non-wood materials, and we'll discuss how to ensure that the basic structure of your deck is supporting the deck as well as it should be.

In this chapter:
- Cleaning, Sealing + Coloring a Wood Deck
- Finishing a New Wood Deck
- Maintaining a Deck
- Repairing a Deck
- Cleaning Vinyl + Composite Decking

Cleaning, Sealing + Coloring a Wood Deck

Whenever you finish or refinish your wood deck, there are three objectives: cleaning the wood, protecting it, and creating the color you want. First, you need to clean the wood or remove the previous finish to prepare for applying new finish. Otherwise, the stain or sealer may not penetrate and bond properly. Second, a protective topcoat of stain or a sealer-preservative weatherizes the wood, limiting its ability to absorb water. Water absorption leads to rot and invites mildew and algae growth that can prematurely damage the finish. The topcoat also helps to block out ultraviolet sunlight, which will fade wood's natural color, age the finish, and dry out the wood until it cracks or splits. The third goal of finishing is the most obvious: staining allows you to change the wood color and either hide the wood grain or enhance it, depending on the product you choose.

If you think of finishing products in terms of cleaning, weatherizing, and coloring, you'll have an easier time choosing the right products for your wood deck-finishing project. Here is an overview of each category of finishing product.

Before

After

Deck Cleaner

If your deck's current finish has faded or the wood has algae or mildew growth, use a deck cleaner to remove the stubborn stains. Deck cleaner will restore gray, weathered wood back to its original color. It will remove general dirt and grime as well as grease spots left by grilling. If the deck is just dirty but not weathered, try using a dilute solution of ordinary dish soap, followed by a good scrubbing. Soap may be all the cleaning agent your deck really needs.

Waterproofing Sealer

Oil-based waterproofing sealers and wood finishes penetrate the wood, carrying silicone or wax additives that keep wood from absorbing water. Most sealers contain mildewcides and UV inhibitors for added protection. Use a waterproofing sealer when you want to preserve the natural color and grain of the wood. Some products will impart a bit of tinting and color, but generally a sealer will leave the wood looking natural when it dries. Unlike stains, sealers have little or no pigment to ward off fading from sunlight. You'll need to reapply a sealer every one to two years to maintain UV protection. Check the manufacturer's specifications on the can.

Semitransparent Stain

Semitransparent stains offer protective qualities similar to waterproofing sealer, but with more pigment added to help the wood resist fading. The more obvious purpose of the pigment, however, is to color the wood or blend different wood tones without obscuring the grain pattern. These stains are oil-based and penetrating, but they do not form a film on the wood's surface. They're a better choice for decking, benches, and horizontal surfaces than solid-color stains, because they won't peel. Plan to reapply every two to four years.

Solid-color Stain

Solid-color stain contains much more pigment than semitransparent stain, and the formulation is closer to thinned paint than to stain. If you want to completely hide wood grain, a solid-color stain is the right choice for the job. It's a blend of oil and latex or latex only, so the stain forms a film on the wood surface instead of penetrating it. As long as the film doesn't peel or crack, it provides superior protection against both water and UV degradation. However, it doesn't stand up to foot traffic as well as oil-based stain. Solid-color stains can be blended in thousands of paint colors. The finish can last five years or more, but generally it will need to be stripped or sanded first before recoating. Avoid using solid-color stain on redwood or cedar. These woods contain tannins and resins that can bleed through the stain and leave spots.

Finishing a New Wood Deck

Finish a new deck with clear sealer-preservative or staining sealer. Sealer-preservatives protect wood from water and rot, and are often used on cedar or redwood because they preserve the original color of the wood. If you want the wood to look weathered, wait several months before applying sealer-preservative.

Staining sealers, sometimes called toners, are often applied to pressure-treated lumber to give it the look of redwood or cedar. Staining sealers are available in a variety of colors.

For best protection, use finishing products with an alkyd base. Apply fresh finish each year.

TOOLS + MATERIALS

Orbital sander
Sandpaper
Shop vacuum
Pressure sprayer
Ear and eye protection
Paintbrush

Clear sealer-preservative
   or staining sealer
Work gloves
Respirator
Goggles

PREPARING THE DECK

Use an orbital sander to smooth out any rough areas before applying finish. Wear a respirator and goggles. Don't sand pressure-treated decking because the chemicals used to preserve the wood are toxic. Simply wash the deck and allow to dry before applying a finish.

A hand-pump style sprayer is inexpensive and speeds up the finish application process.

How to Finish a Redwood or Cedar Deck

Test the wood surface by sprinkling water on it. If the wood absorbs water quickly, it is ready to be sealed. If it doesn't, let the wood dry for several weeks before sealing.

Sand rough areas and vacuum the deck. Apply clear sealer to all wood surfaces, using a pressure sprayer. If possible, apply sealer to the underside of decking and to joists, beams, and posts.

Use a paintbrush to work sealer into cracks, joints, seams, and other areas that could trap water.

 # How to Finish a Pressure-treated Deck

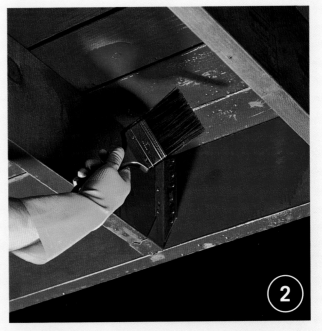

Sand rough areas and vacuum the deck. Apply a staining sealer (toner) to all deck wood using a pressure sprayer.

Use a paintbrush to smooth out drips and runs. Porous wood may require a second coat of staining sealer for even coverage.

NOTE: Sanding older pressure-treated wood is not advisable because of the toxic chemicals in the wood. Any time you cut or sand pressure-treated wood, wear a respirator.

Maintaining a Deck

Inspect your deck at least once a year, more often if the weather over any given season is especially severe. Replace loose or rusting hardware or fasteners as soon as you detect them to prevent future problems. Apply a new coat of sealant as necessary, according to the requirements of the type of wood or other material used in your deck.

Carefully inspect the deck surface, railings, and structure for signs of damage. Replace or reinforce damaged wood as soon as possible. Replace damaged composite decking if it is split or otherwise compromised.

Restore an older, weathered deck to its original wood color and luster with a deck-brightening product. Brighteners are available at most hardware stores and home centers.

NOTE: Even the sharpest DIYer cannot spot many signs that a deck has developed dangerous structural issues. Especially if your deck is more than ten years old, hire a professional deck inspector to examine it.

Inspect the entire deck, including underneath. Look for signs of rot, damage, or wear. Apply a sealant or new finish regularly, as required for the wood in your deck.

TOOLS + MATERIALS

Flashlight	Screwgun	Scrub brush	Eye protection	2½" deck screws
Awl or screwdriver	Putty knife	Rubber gloves	Pressure sprayer	Deck brightener

Maintaining an Older Deck

Use an awl or screwdriver to check the deck for soft, rotted wood. Replace or reinforce damaged wood.

Clean debris from cracks between decking boards with a putty knife. Debris traps moisture and can cause wood to rot.

Drive new fasteners to secure loose decking to joists. If using the old nail or screw holes, new fasteners should be slightly longer than the originals.

How to Renew a Deck

Mix deck-cleaning solution as directed by the manufacturer. Apply the solution with a pressure sprayer and let it set for

Scrub the deck thoroughly with a stiff scrub brush. Wear rubber gloves and eye protection.

Rinse the deck with clear water. If necessary, apply a second coat of cleaner to extremely dirty or stained areas. Rinse and let dry. Apply a fresh coat of sealer or stain.

 ## POWER WASHING

An alternative to hand scrubbing a deck, power washing can be an economical way to clean and prepare even a large deck for sealant in the space of a few hours. Inexpensive home power washers don't always have enough power to completely strip the accumulated coating of dirt and debris off a deck. Instead, rent a gas-powered unit from a local rental center. Use a medium number 2 or 3 nozzle and hold the jet of water about 4 to 6" off the surface of the wood. You can easily clean to the bare wood with one slow pass. Apply a sealant-protectant as soon as the wood dries. Do not use too much water pressure, however, as that may damage the wood.

Repairing a Deck

Replace or reinforce damaged deck wood as soon as possible. Wood rot can spread and weaken solid wood.

After replacing or reinforcing the rotted wood, clean the entire deck and apply a fresh coat of clear sealer-preservative or staining sealer. Apply a fresh coat of finish each year to prevent future water damage. If you need to repair more than a few small areas, it is probably time to replace the entire deck.

How to Repair Damaged Decking + Joists

Remove nails or screws from the damaged decking board if you can. Remove the damaged board.

Inspect the underlying joists for signs of rotted wood. Joists with discolored, soft areas should be repaired and reinforced.

Use a mallet and chisel to remove any rotted portions of the joist.

Apply a coat of sealer-preservative to the damaged joist. Let it dry, then apply a second coat of sealer. Cut a reinforcing joist (sister joist) from pressure-treated lumber.

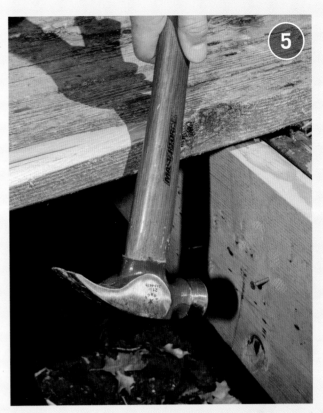

Position the sister joist tightly against the damaged joist, and fasten it in place with 10d nails or screws driven every 12".

Joist hanger location

Attach the sister joist to the ledger and the header joist. Cut replacement decking boards from matching lumber using a metal joist hanger. You may tack the joist in place with a nail prior to installing the hangers.

If the existing decking is gray, "weather" the new decking by scrubbing it with a solution made from 1 cup baking soda and 1 gallon of warm water. Rinse and let dry.

(continued)

Apply a coat of sealer-preservative or staining sealer to all sides of the new decking boards.

Position the new boards and fasten them to the joists with galvanized deck screws. Make sure the space between boards matches that of the existing decking.

 ## How to Replace a Post on a Low Deck

Build a support using plywood scraps, a concrete block, and a hydraulic jack. Place plywood between the head of the jack and the beam. Apply just enough pressure to lift the beam slightly.

NOTE: Because of code revisions, you may be required to replace old posts with larger lumber. Check with your local building department.

Remove any nails or screws holding the damaged post to the post anchor or anchor pad and to the beam. Remove the damaged post and anchor pad or post anchor. Clean the concrete pier of any debris.

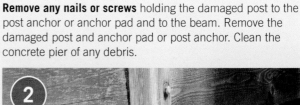

3

If an anchor pad was previously used, use a drill and ⅜"
masonry bit to drill a hole in the concrete pier. Insert a
⅜" masonry anchor. If the post was held in place by a
metal post anchor, you may be able to use the existing hole.

4

Position a galvanized post anchor on the pier block, and
thread a ⅜" lag screw with washer through the hole in the
anchor and into the masonry anchor. Tighten the screw with
a ratchet wrench.

5

Cut a new post from pressure-treated lumber, and treat the
cut ends with sealer-preservative. Position the post and make
sure it is plumb.

6

Attach the bottom of the post to the post anchor using the
recommended fasteners. Attach the post to the beam by
redriving the lag screws, using a ratchet wrench. Release
the pressure on the jack and remove the temporary support.

How to Repair Popped Decking Nails

The cure for most popped nails is simply to remove the nail. Use a nail extractor, cat's paw, or a claw hammer, using a scrap of wood or other protective surface to limit damage to the deck surface. Once the nail is removed, drive a 3" galvanized deck screw down through the nail hole.

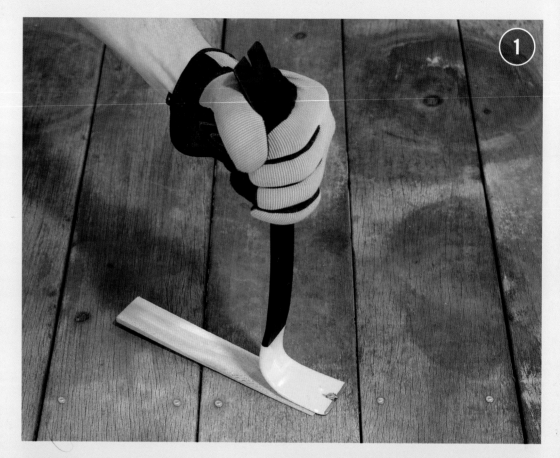

Where a nail has come loose from the joist below, but the head is still securely buried in the board, digging the popped nail out would damage the board. Instead, drive a 3" galvanized deck screw right next to the nail, so that the screw head overlaps the nail head.

How to Reface a Rotted Deck Edge

1

Measure the deck overhang from the joist outward. Decide how far back you want to cut the edge of the deck (usually about ½" to ¾" less than the measurement from the joist).

2

Transfer that measurement to the two end boards on the deck. Drive nails into the boards and snap a chalk line between them to create the cut line.

3

Use a circular saw to cut along the chalk line. Depending on how much you've cut off and what type of material the decking is, you may need to seal the ends with a waterproof sealer-preservative.

4

Cut a cedar, redwood, or pressure treated 1 × 2 to length to cover the edges. Scarf any joints that are necessary along the edging. Use 2½" galvanized deck screws to fasten the 2 × 2 in place. As an alternative, you can stain the 2 × 2 edging in a contrasting shade from the deck and seal it before fastening to the edge.

Cleaning Vinyl + Composite Decking

Vinyl, recycled plastic, aluminum, and composite decking may be easier to maintain and is often more durable than solid wood, but these materials aren't completely exempt from a bit of cosmetic cleanup now and again. Nonwood decking will get dirty and stained in the course of normal use, and you'll need to use different cleaning products, depending on the type of stain. Although it may be tempting to pull out the pressure washer and give your deck a good going over, pressure washers can harm some types of synthetic decking and may even void your deck warranty (check with the manufacturer of your particular decking). A little elbow grease and the right cleaners are often a better approach. Here are suggestions for cleaning various types of stains and marks from vinyl, plastic, or composite decking. Be sure to wear safety glasses and protective gloves when working with strong chemicals.

Dirt + tree sap: Remove ordinary residue from foot traffic, bird droppings, or tree sap with household dish soap diluted with water. Mix a strong concentration in a bucket, scrub the stains, and rinse with clean water.

Fastener, leaf, or tannin: Steel fasteners, tree leaves, or resin stains from cedar or redwood can leave dark tannin stains on composite decking. To remove these, spray on a deck brightener/cleaner product that contains oxalic or phosphoric acid, then flush the surface with lots of fresh water.

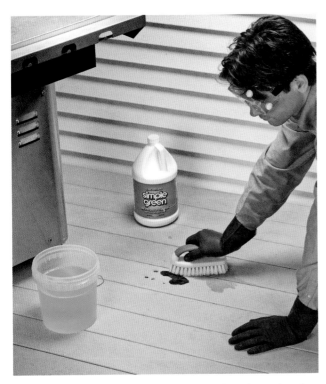

Oil + grease: Oil and grease spots from barbecuing or tanning lotions should be cleaned immediately, before they dry. Use a household degreaser (such as an orange citrus cleaner), Simple Green, or ammonia and a scrub brush to remove the stain. Follow with soapy water and thorough rinsing.

Mold + mildew: Use a mildew and stain remover formulated specifically for use on composites or PVC decking to kill off mold and mildew growth. A good preventive measure is to scrub and wash your deck at least once a season, especially in shady or damp areas where mold and mildew are likely to grow.

Berry + wine: Use a dilute solution of household bleach and water to spot-clean wine or berry stains from decking (only after checking manufacturer's recommendations to ensure the solution won't damage the decking). Depending on the depth of the stain, you may not be able to remove it entirely, but generally these stains will fade over time.

Crayon + marker: If you have young kids, sooner or later crayon or marker stains are inevitable. The trick to removing them is using the correct solvent. Mineral spirits will remove crayon wax, and soapy water cleans up water-based marker stains. Use denatured alcohol (available at home centers) to remove dye-based, permanent markers.

How to Stop Deck Sway

Measure 24" down from where the post meets the beam. Clearly mark that point on the post.

Measure 24" from one edge of the post out along the beam. Mark that point on the beam. Repeat on the other side of the beam. Measure from the mark on the beam to the mark on the post. Add 4" for the total length of the brace.

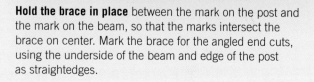

Hold the brace in place between the mark on the post and the mark on the beam, so that the marks intersect the brace on center. Mark the brace for the angled end cuts, using the underside of the beam and edge of the post as straightedges.

Top: Use a miter saw to make the angled end cuts. Place the brace in position and drill top and bottom pilot holes (two at each location), and then screw the brace to the post and beam using 6" lag screws. **Bottom:** Fasten the brace to the underlying deck joists by drilling pilot holes through the post and into the brace and securing again with carriage bolts.

How to Stiffen a Spongy Deck

Measure the space between joists. Use this measurement to cut blocking from pressure treated lumber the same size as the joists. Snap a chalkline down the center of the joists' span. A more permanent (but much more expensive and difficult) solution is to add new intermediate joists.

Tap the blocking in place, positioning blocks in an alternating pattern with one block to the left and one to the right of the chalk line.

Screw through the joists into the end of the blocks on each side using 3" galvanized decking screws.

Deckbuilding Glossary

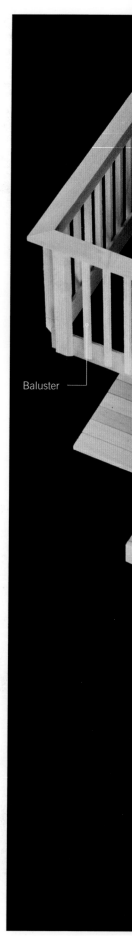

Baluster

Baluster — a vertical railing member.

Batterboards — temporary stake structures used for positioning layout strings.

Beam — the main horizontal support for the deck, usually made from a pair of 2 × 8s or 2 × 10s attached to the deck posts.

Blocking — short pieces of lumber cut from joist material and fastened between joists for reinforcement.

Cap — the topmost horizontal railing member.

Cantilever — a common construction method (employed in some of the deck plans in this book) that involves extending the joists beyond the beam. The maximum overhang is specified in the building code.

Corner-post design — a construction method that incorporates posts at the outside edges of the deck, so the joists do not overhang the beam.

Dead load — the weight of the materials used to build the deck. Usually expressed in pounds per square foot (psf).

Decking — the floor boards of a deck (also known as deck boards).

Face board — attractive wood, usually redwood or cedar, used to cover the rim joists and end joists.

Footing — a concrete component that extends below the frost line and that bears the weight of the deck and transmits the load to the soil.

Horizontal span — the horizontal distance a stairway covers.

Inset — an area of a deck that has been cut out to accommodate landscape features such as trees or to provide access to fixtures.

Joist — dimensional lumber, set on edge, that supports decking. Joists on attached decks hang between the ledger and rim joist.

Joist hanger — metal connecting pieces used to attach joists to ledger or header joists so that top edges are flush.

Ledger — a board, equal in size to the joists, that anchors the deck to the house and supports one end of the joists.

Live load — the anticipated weight of how the deck will be used, including the weight of people, furniture, planters, and the like. Usually expressed in pounds per square foot (psf).

Open step — a step composed of treads mounted between stair stringers without any risers.

Post — a vertical member that supports a deck, stairway, or railing.

Post anchors — also called post bases. Metal hardware for attaching deck posts to footings and raising the bottom of the post to keep it away from water. The end grain itself can be protected with sealer as added protection from rot.

Rim joist — a board fastened to the end of the joists, typically at the opposite end from the ledger. Rim joists attach to both ends of a free-standing deck. The outer (side) joists on a deck platform are also considered rim joists.

Rise — the height of a step.

Riser — a vertical board attached to the front of a step between treads.

Run — the depth of a step.

Span limit — the distance a board can safely cross between supports.

Stair cleat — supports for treads that are attached to stair stringers.

Stair stringer — an inclined member that supports a stairway's treads. A stair stringer may be solid, with treads attached to cleats mounted on the inside face or cut out, with treads resting on top of the cutouts.

Tread — the horizontal face of each step in a stairway, often composed of two 2 × 6 boards.

Vertical drop — the vertical distance from the deck surface to the ground.

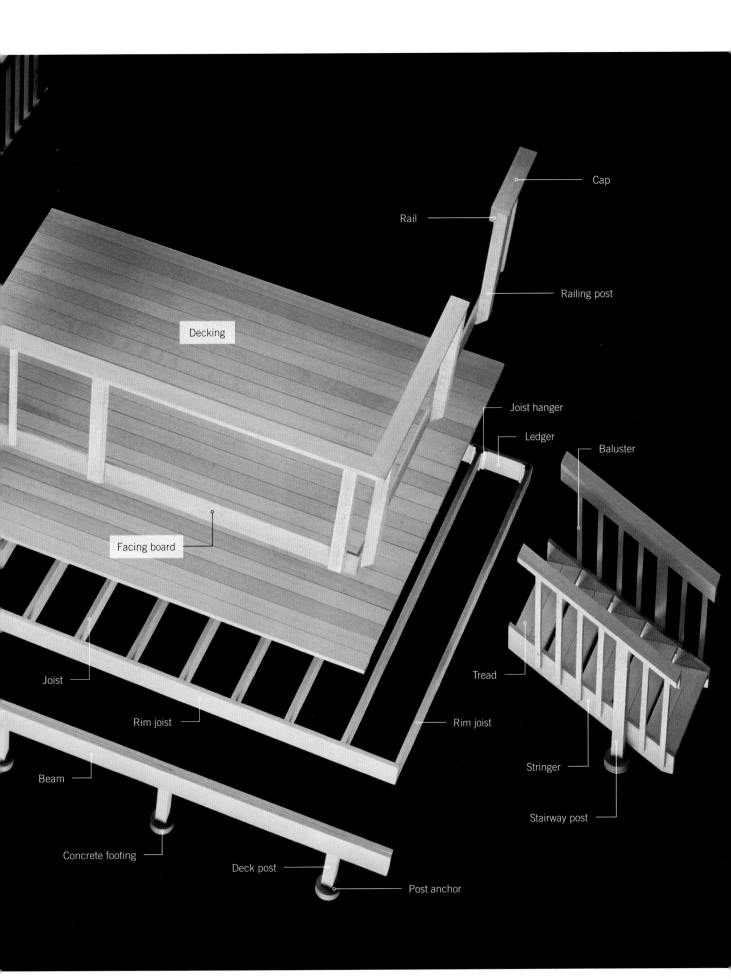

Cap

Rail

Railing post

Decking

Joist hanger

Ledger

Baluster

Facing board

Joist

Tread

Rim joist

Rim joist

Beam

Stringer

Stairway post

Concrete footing

Deck post

Post anchor

Metric Conversions

ENGLISH TO METRIC

TO CONVERT:	TO:	MULTIPLY BY:
Inches	Millimeters	25.4
Inches	Centimeters	2.54
Feet	Meters	0.305
Yards	Meters	0.914
Square inches	Square centimeters	6.45
Square feet	Square meters	0.093
Square yards	Square meters	0.836
Ounces	Milliliters	30.0
Pints (U.S.)	Liters	0.473 (Imp. 0.568)
Quarts (U.S.)	Liters	0.946 (Imp. 1.136)
Gallons (U.S.)	Liters	3.785 (Imp. 4.546)
Ounces	Grams	28.4
Pounds	Kilograms	0.454

TO CONVERT:	TO:	MULTIPLY BY:
Millimeters	Inches	0.039
Centimeters	Inches	0.394
Meters	Feet	3.28
Meters	Yards	1.09
Square centimeters	Square inches	0.155
Square meters	Square feet	10.8
Square meters	Square yards	1.2
Milliliters	Ounces	.033
Liters	Pints (U.S.)	2.114 (Imp. 1.76)
Liters	Quarts (U.S.)	1.057 (Imp. 0.88)
Liters	Gallons (U.S.)	0.264 (Imp. 0.22)
Grams	Ounces	0.035
Kilograms	Pounds	2.2

CONVERTING TEMPERATURES

Convert degrees Fahrenheit (F) to degrees Celsius (C) by following this simple formula: Subtract 32 from the Fahrenheit temperature reading. Then multiply that number by $\frac{5}{9}$. For example, 77°F - 32 = 45. 45 × $\frac{5}{9}$ = 25°C.

To convert degrees Celsius to degrees Fahrenheit, multiply the Celsius temperature reading by $\frac{9}{5}$. Then, add 32. For example, 25°C × $\frac{9}{5}$ = 45. 45 + 32 = 77°F.

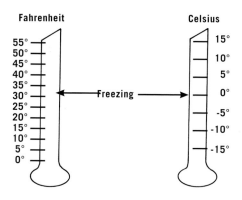

METRIC PLYWOOD PANELS

Metric plywood panels are commonly available in two sizes: 1,200 mm × 2,400 mm and 1,220 mm × 2,400 mm, which is roughly equivalent to a 4 × 8-ft. sheet. Standard and Select sheathing panels come in standard thicknesses, while Sanded grade panels are available in special thicknesses.

STANDARD SHEATHING GRADE		SANDED GRADE	
7.5 mm	($\frac{5}{16}$ in.)	6 mm	($\frac{4}{17}$ in.)
9.5 mm	($\frac{3}{8}$ in.)	8 mm	($\frac{5}{16}$ in.)
12.5 mm	($\frac{1}{2}$ in.)	11 mm	($\frac{7}{16}$ in.)
15.5 mm	($\frac{5}{8}$ in.)	14 mm	($\frac{9}{16}$ in.)
18.5 mm	($\frac{3}{4}$ in.)	17 mm	($\frac{2}{3}$ in.)
20.5 mm	($\frac{13}{16}$ in.)	19 mm	($\frac{3}{4}$ in.)
22.5 mm	($\frac{7}{8}$ in.)	21 mm	($\frac{13}{16}$ in.)
25.5 mm	(1 in.)	24 mm	($\frac{15}{16}$ in.)

LUMBER DIMENSIONS

NOMINAL - U.S.	ACTUAL - U.S. (IN INCHES)	METRIC
1 × 2	¾ × 1½	19 × 38 mm
1 × 3	¾ × 2½	19 × 64 mm
1 × 4	¾ × 3½	19 × 89 mm
1 × 5	¾ × 4½	19 × 114 mm
1 × 6	¾ × 5½	19 × 140 mm
1 × 7	¾ × 6¼	19 × 159 mm
1 × 8	¾ × 7¼	19 × 184 mm
1 × 10	¾ × 9¼	19 × 235 mm
1 × 12	¾ × 11¼	19 × 286 mm
1¼ × 4	1 × 3½	25 × 89 mm
1¼ × 6	1 × 5½	25 × 140 mm
1¼ × 8	1 × 7¼	25 × 184 mm
1¼ × 10	1 × 9¼	25 × 235 mm
1¼ × 12	1 × 11¼	25 × 286 mm
1½ × 4	1¼ × 3½	32 × 89 mm
1½ × 6	1¼ × 5½	32 × 140 mm
1½ × 8	1¼ × 7¼	32 × 184 mm
1½ × 10	1¼ × 9¼	32 × 235 mm
1½ × 12	1¼ × 11¼	32 × 286 mm
2 × 4	1½ × 3½	38 × 89 mm
2 × 6	1½ × 5½	38 × 140 mm
2 × 8	1½ × 7¼	38 × 184 mm
2 × 10	1½ × 9¼	38 × 235 mm
2 × 12	1½ × 11¼	38 × 286 mm
3 × 6	2½ × 5½	64 × 140 mm
4 × 4	3½ × 3½	89 × 89 mm
4 × 6	3½ × 5½	89 × 140 mm

LIQUID MEASUREMENT EQUIVALENTS

1 Pint	= 16 Fluid Ounces	= 2 Cups
1 Quart	= 32 Fluid Ounces	= 2 Pints
1 Gallon	= 128 Fluid Ounces	= 4 Quarts

COUNTERBORE, SHANK + PILOT HOLE DIAMETERS

SCREW SIZE	COUNTERBORE DIAMETER FOR SCREW HEAD (IN INCHES)	CLEARANCE HOLE FOR SCREW SHANK (IN INCHES)	PILOT HOLE DIAMETER	
			HARD WOOD (IN INCHES)	SOFT WOOD (IN INCHES)
#1	.146 (9/64)	5/64	3/64	1/32
#2	1/4	3/32	3/64	1/32
#3	1/4	7/64	1/16	3/64
#4	1/4	1/8	1/16	3/64
#5	1/4	1/8	5/64	1/16
#6	5/16	9/64	3/32	5/64
#7	5/16	5/32	3/32	5/64
#8	3/8	11/64	1/8	3/32
#9	3/8	11/64	1/8	3/32
#10	3/8	3/16	1/8	7/64
#11	1/2	3/16	5/32	9/64
#12	1/2	7/32	9/64	1/8

NAILS

Nail lengths are identified by numbers from 4 to 60 followed by the letter "d," which stands for "penny." For general framing and repair work, use common or box nails. Common nails are best suited to framing work where strength is important. Box nails are smaller in diameter than common nails, which makes them easier to drive and less likely to split wood. Use box nails for light work and thin materials. Most common and box nails have a cement or vinyl coating that improves their holding power.

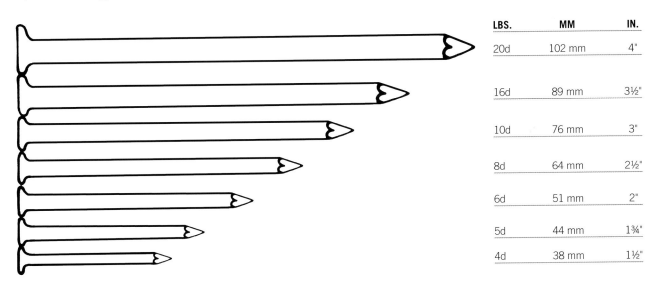

LBS.	MM	IN.
20d	102 mm	4"
16d	89 mm	3½"
10d	76 mm	3"
8d	64 mm	2½"
6d	51 mm	2"
5d	44 mm	1¾"
4d	38 mm	1½"

Resources

American Wood Council
Design and construction
guidance in building wood
structures.
(202) 463-2766
www.awc.org

Azek
Composite decking.
(877) ASK-AZEK
www.azek.com

Bison Innovative Products
Deck screwjack pedestals and
modular decking systems
for rooftops and backyard.
(800) 333-4234
www.bisonip.com

BLACK + DECKER
Portable power tools and more.
(800) 544-6986
www.blackanddecker.com

Deck-A-Floor
Modular decking system for
flat surfaces.
www.newtechwood.com

Deckorators
Decorative deck railings,
balusters, post caps,
decking, and lighting.
www.deckorators.com

Dekmate
Prefab braces for deck
benches
www.2x4basics.com/
dekmate-products

Duralife
Composite decking and
railings.
(800) 866-8101
www.duralifedecking.com

Feeney Architectural
Steel railing cables, railing
frame systems.
(800) 888-2418
www.feeneyinc.com

Fiberon
Composite decking,
railing, deck lighting,
and fasteners.
(800) 573-8841
www.fiberondecking.com

**DuxxBak Decking (formerly
Green Bay Decking)**
Manufacturer of GeoDeck
decking and railing.
www.duxxbakdecking.com

Architrex (formerly HandyDeck)
Deck tiles.
(866) 206-8316
www.archatrak.com

LB Plastics
Synthetic railings, decking,
and accessories.
(704) 663-1543
www.lbplastics.com

TimberTech
Composite decking, railing,
and accessories.
(877) 275-2935
www.timbertech.com

Trex
Composite decking, railing,
and accessories.
(800) BUY-TREX
www.trex.com

Underdeck
Underdeck enclosure and
drainage system.
(570) 345-6600
www.underdeck.com

Versadeck
Aluminum decking and
modular deck system.
(651) 356-1870
www.versadeck.com

Photo Credits

Absolute Concrete: 223 (top right), 224 (bottom left)

AZEK, azek.com, (877) ASK-AZEK: 11 (top right), 16 (top left)

California Redwood Association, www.calredwood.org

   Ernest Braun: 10 (top right), 17 (top left)

Capital: 220, 224 (bottom right)

CertainTeed Corporation: 11 (bottom)

Clemens Jellema, Fine Decks, Inc., www.finedecks.com: 12 (top),
13 (bottom), 17 (top right)

Consentino: 224 (top left)

Deckorators: 14 (top left), 159 (top left, middle right, bottom two)

Decks by Kiefer, www.decksbykiefer.com, designs@decksbykiefer.com:
17 (bottom)

Distinctive Design: 21 (top left), 159 (top right and middle left)

**DuraLife™ Decking & Railing Systems, www.duralifedecking.com,
(800) 866-8101:** 14 (bottom)

GeoDeck: 16 (bottom), 219 (top right)

HandyDeck: 219 (top left)

iStock: 21 (bottom right)

**Jay Graham (Design: Gary Marsh Design LLC; Construction: All Decked
Out, Novato, CA):** 8, 13 (top right), 15 (middle left)

Joseph Truini Photographer: 26 (bottom), 51 (bottom left), 115, 116,
146, 147 (bottom), 228, 229

Shutterstock: 10 (top left), 12 (bottom), 13 (top left), 14 (top right),
15 (top), 15 (middle right), 16 (top right), 30, 97 (bottom), 137
(bottom), 166

Simpson Strong-Tie, www.strongtie.com: 38 (both)

TAMKO Building Products, Inc., www.evergrain.com: 21 (top right)

Trex Company, Inc.: 6, 10 (bottom), 11 (top left), 15 (bottom), 20,
21 (bottom left)

Viking: 218, 219 (bottom), 221 (bottom right), 222

Index